D0078755

SILENCE TO THE DRUMS

CONTRIBUTIONS IN AFRO-AMERICAN
AND AFRICAN STUDIES

S
53
N5
4

SILENCE TO THE DRUMS

A SURVEY OF THE LITERATURE OF THE HARLEM RENAISSANCE

MARGARET PERRY

CONTRIBUTIONS IN AFRO-AMERICAN AND AFRICAN STUDIES, NUMBER 18

GREENWOOD PRESS
WESTPORT, CONN.
LONDON, ENGLAND

Tennessee Tech. Library
Cookeville, Tenn.

288918

Library of Congress Cataloging in Publication Data

Perry, Margaret, 1933-
Silence to the drums.

(Contributions in Afro-American and African studies ; no. 18)
Bibliography: p.
Includes index.
1. American literature—Negro authors—History and criticism.
2. American literature—20th century—History and criticism. I. Title.
II. Series.
PS153.N5P4   810'.9'896   74-19806
ISBN 0-8371-7847-9

Copyright © 1976 by Margaret Perry

All rights reserved. No portion of this book may be reproduced, by any
process or technique, without the express written consent of the publisher.

Library of Congress Catalog Card Number: 74-19806
ISBN: 0-8371-7847-9

First published in 1976
Second printing 1977

Greenwood Press, Inc.
51 Riverside Avenue, Westport, Connecticut 06880

Printed in the United States of America

*   *   *

Grateful acknowledgment is extended to Alfred A. Knopf, Inc., for
permission to quote from the following copyrighted works of
Langston Hughes: *The Weary Blues, Selected Poems,* and *The Panther
and the Lash.*

Grateful acknowledgment is given to the following individuals and publishers for permission to reprint:

To Waring Cuney for "No Images."

To Anne Spencer for extracts from her poems, "Life-Long Poor Browning," "Lines for a Nasturtium," "For Jim, Easter Eve," and "At the Carnival."

To Sterling A. Brown for extracts from "Foreclosure," Slim Greer," and "Strong Men" in *Southern Road.* Copyright © 1932 by Sterling A. Brown. And for extract from "When De Saints Go Ma'chin Home" in *American Negro Poetry* by Arna Bontemps (1963).

To the Estate of Frank S. Horne for extract from "Letter Found Near a Suicide."

Excerpts from "Go Down Death—A Funeral Sermon," "The Crucifixion," and "Let My People Go" from *God's Trombones* by James Weldon Johnson. Copyright 1927 by the Viking Press, Inc. Copyright © renewed 1955 by Grace Nail Johnson. Reprinted by permission of The Viking Press.

Extracts from "The Return" and "God Give to Men" by Arna Bontemps in *Personals* published by Paul Breman 1963. Reprinted by permission of Harold Ober Associates, Incorporated. Copyright © 1963 by Arna Bontemps.

Extracts from "The Shroud of Color," "Yet Do I Marvel," "A Song of Praise," and "Heritage" from *On These I Stand* by Countee Cullen (1947). Reprinted by permission of Harper & Row, publisher, and Mrs. Ida M. Cullen.

Extract from *Cane* by Jean Toomer. Copyright © 1951 by Jean Toomer. Reprinted by permission of Liveright, Publishers, New York.

Extracts from *Selected Poems of Claude McKay.* Reprinted by permission of Twayne Publishers, Inc., Boston.

Quotation from letter of Countee Cullen to Harold Jackman, 1 July 1923, used by permission of the James Weldon Johnson Memorial Collection, Collection of American Literature, Beinecke Rare Book and Manuscript Library, Yale University; and by permission of Mrs. Ida M. Cullen.

Dedicated to the Memory of the Late
Arna W. Bontemps
(1902-1973)
and
to My Eldest Godchild,
Margaret Elizabeth Sullivan

Oh let us go back and search the tangled dream
And as the muffled drum-beats throb and miss
Remember again how early darkness comes
To dreams and silence to the drums.
ARNA BONTEMPS, "THE RETURN"

CONTENTS

ACKNOWLEDGEMENTS

The writer wishes to acknowledge several people and organizations for aid in her research and writing:

The University of Rochester Administration and the University of Rochester Library Administration for summer leave in order to write the first draft of the manuscript.

The library staffs of the Beinecke Library (Yale), Schomburg Collection (New York Public Library), and George Arents Library (Syracuse).

To Ellen Cronk, my typist.

To N. V. G. for her invaluable aid at certain phases of my work.

And to my copy editors, Betty Pessagno and Ann Santoro.

Margaret Perry
University of Rochester
Rochester, New York

INTRODUCTION

In 1925 Arthur A. Schomburg wrote, "The American Negro must remake his past in order to make his future."[1] This statement can serve to accentuate a significant movement in early twentieth-century American literature—the "Harlem Renaissance," or, as Alain Locke, one of the mentors of this movement, called it at its inception, the "Negro Renaissance." But Harlem, the "Mecca of the New Negro," was a primary influence; as Langston Hughes pointed out: "Harlem was like a great magnet for the Negro intellectual, pulling him from everywhere."[2] During a 1970 interview, Arna Bontemps also stated that "Harlem [as the movement's appellation] identifies it more precisely . . . gave it unity . . . located it in time and place."[3] This book, therefore, will serve as a survey of black writers who rose to fame or appeared in print with some regularity during the 1920s and who, with few exceptions, burned themselves out by the mid-1930s when the proletarian writers, both black and white, took over.

The revolt of young black writers which took place in the 1960s and 1970s is no great phenomenon in the literary world. In addition, the interest in blackness, the "Afro" part of the black man in America, is not as recent as the media might have one believe. A call for the emancipation of the black man's spirit was loud and vociferous even before 1920. The seeds for the present unrest and disaffection were planted in the 1920s. The current flowering of Afro-Americanism is simply a resuscitation of an older and sometimes exotic flower.

The Harlem Renaissance, unique in ways that will be explored later, occurred at a period when other literary and artistic movements were in existence—the whole lost generation, or the Bloomsbury group, for example—but there was an element of isolationism about the Harlem Renaissance movement. This was partially racial: blacks felt a great need to discover their roots, and the emphasis on Afro-Americanism limited the coterie to all but a few outside the black race. The white man brought his past with him and gradually shed it in the process of becoming completely Americanized. The black man, deracinated, separated not only from his former culture but also from his immediate family, had to find out not only what he was but what he had been. This, in part, resulted in a literature that was a mélange of atavistic racial propaganda and black bourgeois romanticism. Its analogue can be seen in any displaced people who have advanced to the time and place in their "new" history that necessitates an appraisal of the past and of the self.

The search for the roots of the black man's being and the glorification of blackness were only part of the artist's problem during the Harlem Renaissance. The intellectuals who created this movement—writers, poets, and novelists—were also concerned with the universal artistic purpose: to transform experience into art. In the case of these black writers, the object was to communicate sentiments as well as experience, for the black writer did not want to lose what he felt to be part of his uniqueness: his ability to feel deeply and his pride in exhibiting his emotions. Here, the artists differed from their bourgeois black brothers and sisters who, in striving upward and in achieving what they considered greater "respectability," rejected displaying "the irrepressible exuberance and legendary vitality of the black race."[4] It will be seen, also, that this segment of the black population did not support the writers of the Harlem Renaissance.

The purpose of this book is to scrutinize a decade (give or take a year) of artistic outpourings by black writers. The social and environmental background will be explored briefly, followed by a closer examination of writers and their writings, the high point of these creative activities, and the waning of the movement.

NOTES

1. Arthur A. Schomburg, "The Negro Digs Up His Past," in Alain Locke, ed., *The New Negro* (New York: Boni, 1927, c. 1925), p. 231.
2. Langston Hughes, *The Big Sea* (New York: Hill and Wang, 1963, c. 1940), p. 240.
3. Statement made to the author by Arna Bontemps in a taped interview at Yale University, 18 December 1970.
4. Claude McKay, *Banjo* (New York: Harper, 1929), p. 324.

one
BACKGROUND

Nations are like idealistic and adventuresome youths who go East or West to seek a fortune or a grand opportunity: the return home, for whatever reason, never can resubmerge the wanderer into the true past. The wanderer soon notices, too, that the escape back into the past does not seem as desirable after a little time has elapsed. Nations were in much the same state of mind after the end of World War I. Writers and artists who could see more deeply into their own age noted that the world wasn't much better than it had been prior to the war. The ordinary citizen—in the United States, at least—felt this to be true during the depression that followed the war. The black man was doubly burdened, for he had to contend with the depression more intensely and, in 1919, with race riots.

The black men and women who faced the horrors of the race riots were a different breed of blacks from those who had lived under the yoke of slavery. In a way, the "Great War" was a help to blacks. During this time many blacks migrated to the large cities where more jobs were available (although not as many jobs as the migrating blacks believed were awaiting them); for example, the black population of New York City increased by 66 percent between 1910 and 1920.[1] And, too, the returning black soldier was in no mood to resume a life that attuned itself to the suppressive will of the white man. A white writer noted a conversation he had with one of his black acquaintances:

> No mere fanciful bugaboo is the new negro. He exists. More than once I have met him. He differs radically from the timorous, docile negro of the past. Said a new negro, 'Cap'n, you mark my words; the next time white folks pick on colored folks, something's going to drop—dead white folks.' Within a week came race riots in Chicago, where negroes fought back with surprising audacity.[2]

This was a new world, then, a world not made safe for peace, but nevertheless new. For the black man in Harlem it was a world of simplistic contrasts; it was also a world observed and dissected by the white man. Harlem may have been the "Mecca of the New Negro" but, under its surface, it was also a home for literally thousands of poor blacks who never knew a renaissance came, flowered, and then faded. Here, capsulized, is the Harlem that hosted the young black artists of the 1920s.

It is dangerous to point a finger at one date and say it marks the beginning of a movement, but there was a series of unrelated events that, in retrospect, indicate that the Harlem Renaissance period was developing prior to the 1920s. The production of three plays about Negro life by Ridgely Torrence, presented in New York on 5 April 1917, was an important event because this was the first time a dramatic rendition of black life was handled with a degree of genuine seriousness. The plays (*Granny Maumee, The Rider of Dreams,* and *Simon the Cyrenian*) were not successful, but they were significant. "If the plays did not sound a battle cry they did show an acceptance and a respect that the Negro had not yet been afforded in American society or on the American stage. They were a beginning for the Negro in our theater."[3] The ordinary resident in Harlem was not concerned with these plays, of course. The Harlem of the 1920s was still in a changeable state, although it seemed inevitable by 1915 that Harlem would become a black community. World War I provided an impetus for Negroes to migrate northward where they filled rank-and-file jobs vacated by whites who went to war. Harlem was the prime destination of most of these Negroes. If artists like Mr. Torrence could take Negroes seriously enough to present his plays downtown, the world might also be ready to acknowledge the black man as a real person. It is not surprising to note how unprepared the world of New York was for such a notion. But the war obscured the future significance of the influx of Negroes into New York City. Harlem was "a place" as well as a state of mind by the end of World War I. It was in the process of becoming the "Black Capital" of the United States.

In 1925, when James Weldon Johnson wrote that the character of Harlem was essentially a development of the preceding ten years, he was talking, of course, about black Harlem. At the turn of the century, Harlem began to be "invaded" by some of the wealthier Negroes who were not hampered by its remoteness or the lack of transportation to its tree-lined streets. The houses were beautiful, spacious, and elegant; the Negroes, generally, paid more for these homes than whites simply because of race. Middle-class and then poor blacks followed their richer brethren, and, in classic fashion, the whites fled Harlem (not, however, before attempting to thwart the colorful flow with such tactics as buying up a building in which Negroes resided and then evicting them. The Afro-American Realty Company, formed by Philip A. Payton, "countered by similar methods").[4] As the dark-hued migration continued, the ambiance was transformed by the character of its newer inhabitants. As late as 1924 it was written: "Hundred of negroes arrive daily in New York from every Southern state . . . Yet hundreds find themselves on the street. The Harlem Forum, where many are taken care of out of charity, is overcrowded nightly with shivering, ragged, hungry creatures who look as though they had just escaped hell. There is no way to stop the invasion. There is no way to enlarge the houses in which negroes live. . . . Segregation breeds immorality, criminality, diseases, and increases mortality. . . . Prostitution, bootlegging, and charlatanism are rampant on every corner."[5] This was one side of Harlem. But Harlem, as soon as the black man dotted the scene, was a section of New York City that offered as many contrasts in life-styles as there were shades of blacks.

Philip A. Payton was not the only black real estate dealer in Harlem. There were also John E. Nail (father of Grace Nail, who married James Weldon Johnson), Henry C. Parker "Pig Foot Mary" (Mrs. Mary Dean), and innumerable unknowns who managed to save enough from modest earnings as cooks or washerwomen for a down payment on property.[6] Churches were extensive property owners, too: it was estimated by one writer that "St. Philips has holdings valued at $1,000,000. All told, the Harlem negroes control real estate worth $20,000,000 according to the lowest estimate, $300,000,000 according to the highest."[7] In both style and condition, houses and apartments in this "Mecca of the New Negro" ran the gamut from the dignified brownstones, designed in 1891 by Stanford White, on 139th Street (known as "Striver's Row") to the solid, staid Dunbar Apartments at 150th-151st Streets (between 7th and 8th Avenues), down to the innumerable, nondescript rows of commonplace dwellings locked together row upon row on the streets surrounding Lenox, 7th, and 8th Avenues. In the latter apartments, wedged together like a cluster of migrating birds, there was overcrowding on a monstrous scale. This was part of the economics of keeping alive: all branches of a family, no matter how loosely related, had to live together in order to pay the rent. Those without vast families rented a room or two, or even a hallway, to other poor Negroes. Most ingenious of all, the Harlem rent party was born.

The rent party had its genesis in the Southern habit of arranging a "shindig" when supplementary funds for the family were needed. A small entrance fee was charged and the participants were provided with music for dancing. Food and drinks could be bought for an additional small "contribution," and, depending on the house, a reputation for a food specialty, such as pigs-feet, chitterlings, or hog maws, could be built and thereby assure attendance at subsequent parties. Harlem elaborated on this imported phenomenon until many of these house-rent parties—essentially a necessity because of exorbitant rents and low incomes—could be characterized as miniature clubs. Cards were often printed to advertise the parties, variously termed "social parties" or "whist socials"; as an added inducement, verses were sometimes inscribed: "We got yellow girls, we've got black and tan/ Will you have a good time?—YEAH MAN!"[8] The writers of the Harlem Renaissance describe such parties in their work, in poems as well as in novels and short stories. Despite the quaintness some found in these social gatherings and despite the enjoyment of those who attended them, the truth behind the whole phenomenon was reiterated by Gilbert Osofsky in 1966 when he wrote, "The white world saw rent parties as picturesque affairs—in reality they were a product of economic exploitation and they often degenerated into rowdy, bawdy and violent evenings."[9]

One part of Harlem life that was infrequently depicted in novels and verse was the black man's church (a notable exception, of course, is Cullen's *One Way to Heaven*). Yet this institution was a strong influence in the lives of Negroes and was certainly instrumental in the development of Harlem. Not only did the churches own much of the property in Harlem, but the larger ones also assumed the role of counseling and educational centers for the poor and ill-educated. In his early study of this unique segment of the greater metropolis, James Weldon Johnson wrote: "Indeed, a Negro church is for its members much more besides a place of worship. It is a social centre, it is a club, it is

an arena for the exercise of one's capabilities and powers, a
world in which one may achieve self-realization and prefer-
ment . . . with the Negro all these attributes are magnified because of the fact that they are so curtailed for him in the world
at large."[10]

Other dominant influences in the lives of Negroes in Harlem
were two organizations that remain pervasive in any struggle
concerned with the rights of Negroes: the NAACP and the
National Urban League. Formed within two years of each other
(the NAACP in 1909 and the National Urban League in 1911),
each organization attracted persons who became prominent in
the causes of social, economic, and racial justice for Negroes.
The importance of these two organizations for the writers of
the Harlem Renaissance, however, can be traced to the magazines sponsored by these two agencies. *Opportunity*, published
by the National Urban League from 1924 to 1949, was true
to its goal of stimulating self-expression among younger Negro
writers, for the magazine sponsored numerous poetry and prose
contests. In addition, the editorial staff was responsible for the
publication of *Ebony and Topaz*, a large, oversized book containing a mélange of poetry, stories, sociology, and art. *The
Crisis*, a magazine published under the aegis of the NAACP,
had W. E. B. DuBois as its editor for twenty-three years. Many
works of the Harlem Renaissance writers were published in *The
Crisis*, although its strong emphasis on the black mystique permitted strong and weak literature to appear indiscriminately.
Jessie Fauset was an associate editor for a few years, and she
was a generous friend to many of the young writers whom she
aided and, in some cases, invited to her home as well. *The
Crisis* printed many photographs—for instance, of newly graduated college students—and it is a lesson in itself to browse
through the magazine, viewing the pictures. Both *The Crisis*
and *Opportunity*, as organs for printing the work of the Negro
intelligentsia and literati, were valuable also because of the
influence they exerted on the white community. Both periodi-

cals served to interpret the Negro more realistically for that segment of the white population which was at least willing to acknowledge the black man as a part of American society.

The black bourgeoisie probably received most of its exposure to the young Negro writers through these two magazines, for the black middle class, in general, chose to ignore the Harlem Renaissance. As a class, the black bourgeoisie had just emerged from the kind of world that the writers of the Harlem Renaissance chose to portray and, in some cases, to exalt. Glorifying its African heritage and its primitive spirit was anathema to the evolving black middle class. Therefore, the young writers were a philosophical threat to its new, still faltering security. Yet the writers were people to boast about in the right company, and *The Crisis* and *Opportunity* kept the bourgeoisie informed about the more famous of the new authors.

These magazines (especially *The Crisis*) are also a useful record of the 1919 race riots. It is not too extravagant to say that these riots had an effect on the writers who were to be the significant makers of the Harlem Renaissance. The riots, even those in Washington, D.C., and Chicago, stimulated post-war migration to Harlem which served to reinforce the trend toward creating a true black capital. Reports about the riots not only emphasized the overt injustice of them but also directed attention to the number of blacks who were fighting back. Thus black and white alike were being exposed to a new image of the Negro. The young writer might become known as the "New Negro," but the masses were new in their own way, too. And one person exploited this new racial pride, built it up, nurtured it, and helped to raise it to new heights: Marcus Aurelius Garvey suddenly flashed upon the scene.

Garvey was a dazzler. Opinions pro and con about the man were rarely dispassionate: the masses loved him, the bourgeoisie shunned him, and the intellectuals laughed at his buffoonish antics. Yet Garvey was an important influence on the image that the black man shaped for himself after World War I. Long before today's youth coined the phrase "Black is Beautiful,"

the concept was implanted by this unassimilated black man
from the West Indian island of Jamaica.

There was an aura of romanticism in Garvey's appeal to the
racial heritage, and when he would shout lustily, "Up, you
mighty race!" the response was electric. Garvey collected
thousands of dollars for his dream of "Back to Africa" for all
the blacks in America. His organization was fantastic—the Black
Cross, the Black Legion, the Black Star Line (with two deplor-
able ships), and a host of nobility created by Garvey, who
labeled himself the High Potentate of the U.N.I.A. and "Pro-
visional President of Africa." U.N.I.A. was the acronym for
his organization, the Universal Negro Improvement Association; because of Garvey's insistence upon blackness, some
Negroes derisively called the U.N.I.A. the Ugliest Negroes in
America. Garvey was undaunted, however, because his egotism
knew no bounds and his vision of his future world was unclouded
by any of the practical realities that eventually shattered his
dream. Losses in business ventures and the fact that he was
surrounded by dishonest sycophants made him an easy prey
for the government's charges of fraudulent practices. In 1925
he was found guilty and sentenced to five years in prison. He
spent two years in the Atlanta Federal Penitentiary before he
received a pardon from President Coolidge, who granted it on
condition that Garvey be deported to Jamaica. Garvey continued his socio-political activities there, and later he moved
to London to continue his struggle. Ironically, Garvey never
set foot upon the soil of Africa.

Although Garvey's schemes failed (for one thing, he did not
understand the psyche of the Negro American), he did stimulate
the black man to think about his heritage and to regard himself
as a member of a race with a past worthy of exploring. Garvey
stirred that longing in the black man to recreate his racial past
in a modern mode. The people who gave an active voice to this
sentiment were those who also mocked him and who were
denounced by him in turn—the writers and artists of the Harlem
Renaissance. They might have thought Garvey a fool but they
could appreciate the spirit of his rhetoric.[11]

Another definite influence on both the artistic and racial
spheres of thought and feeling was the production of *Shuffle
Along.* This all-Negro production opened at the 63rd Street
Theatre in 1921 after having been on the road. The book and
the music were by Negroes, the director was a Negro, and the
actors were Negroes. It was a production for a black audience,
and, of course, the white audience loved it. As one drama historian wrote: *"Shuffle Along* did anything but shuffle. It ex-
ploded onto the stage."[12] This show had such songs as "I'm
Just Wild About Harry' and "Love Will Find a Way," and the
star of the show was the immortal Florence Mills.[13] Among
those in the chorus was Josephine Baker. Success was inevitable,
one might speculate. In any case, the show reinforced the notion
that the Negro was an actor and performer not to be ridiculed
but to be admired. A year prior to *Shuffle Along,* Charles
Gilpin had appeared in Eugene O'Neill's *The Emperor Jones*
and had received a Spingarn Medal for his performance. The
Negro artist, then, was one to be reckoned with; he was emerging as a recognizable human being.

The world that the young black writer faced was one of
ambivalence and agitation; old ideals were suspect and, therefore, discredited. The young set a fast pace for living; older
persons sought relief from the high gear that the war years had
imposed. The year 1919 was one of crisis in America: there
was a depression evolving, there were rent strikes in New York
City, the wave of racial intolerance reached a peak (76 lynched,
as opposed to 36 in 1917 and 60 in 1918), and by November
there were approximately two million Americans on strike.
Prices dropped during 1920-1921, driving many businesses into
bankruptcy. But the depression and unemployment, however
real, were short-lived. What troubles the white man had with
existence were disproportionately worse for the black man.

By 1920 the desire to escape all the threats of the past and
to recapture their former "innocence" resulted in the election
of Warren G. Harding as president. His promise of a return to
"normalcy" was as false a hope as its premise. Hoping to avoid

facing their problems, Americans wrapped themselves in a cocoon of self-righteousness. Prohibition came into law in January 1920, there was the Teapot Dome Scandal in 1923, and the craze for the dance marathon started during this same year. By the following year the Ku Klux Klan had political control of seven states. In 1920 *The Age of Innocence, This Side of Paradise,* and *The Four Horsemen of the Apocalypse* were published, followed by *Main Street,* which poked fun at the very people who devoured the book.

This was in part the world outside Harlem—the world that ignored the artistic ferment brewing in the black capital. Many who came to Harlem came in search of the exotic and bizarre. They saw Harlem, in James Weldon Johnson's words, as a playground. The notion of exoticism remained a self-serving characteristic throughout the decade. The world outside Harlem was also one that proclaimed itself the "Jazz Age" and was, in turn, declared by that portly lady in Paris a "lost generation." A bit of this ambience touched the artists of the Harlem Renaissance, for some of the black writers were friends with their white counterparts in this decade of literary overgrowth. However, the important discovery for the black writer during this period was self-revelation and a recapturing of, or quest for, the past heritage that had been stripped from his race. The world outside the black one, the world that still controlled black life in many spheres, was the recipient of a new and distinct literature produced by the "New Negro" during the 1920s. Just as a renaissance is so called because it looks to a past age—in most cases the Hellenic—it is also a period characterized by fresh discoveries and new modes of expression. It is not only a revival, then, but also a reawakening. For the black writer of the 1920s, the leap into the past and the nurturing of the present were tasks surmountable in great part because he was not alone. He was, indeed, a part of a movement, a person caught up in the brotherhood of racial pride and dignity, a person who was in a small universe of individuals on a quest for the racial lifeline that would sustain each one in his literary endeavors.

NOTES

1. Gilbert Osofsky, *Harlem: The Making of a Ghetto* (New York: Harper & Row, 1966), p. 128.

2. Rollin Lynde Hartt, "The New Negro," *The Independent* 105 (15 January 1921): 59.

3. John M. Clum, *Ridgely Torrence* (New York: Twayne, 1972), p. 117.

4. James Weldon Johnson, "The Making of Harlem," *Survey Graphic* 6 (March 1925): 636.

5. Konrad Bercovici, "The Black Blocks of Manhattan," *Harpers Monthly Magazine* 149 (October 1924): 623.

6. Johnson, "The Making of Harlem," p. 637.

7. Rollin Lynde Hartt, "I'd Like to Show You Harlem," *The Independent* 105 (2 April 1921): 335.

8. Langston Hughes, *The Big Sea* (New York: Hill and Wang, c. 1940, 1963), p. 229.

9. Osofsky, *Harlem: The Making of a Ghetto*, p. 139.

10. James Weldon Johnson, *Black Manhattan* (New York: Knopf, 1940), p. 165.

11. Garvey, even though his ranks were filled with the poor and illiterate, did have the support of some influential people, such as Emmet J. Scott and Frederick A. Cullen.

12. Lofton Mitchell, *Black Drama: The Story of the American Negro in the Theatre* (New York: Hawthorn, 1967), p. 76.

13. Born in Washington, D.C., in 1895, Florence Mills was a child prodigy whose career started during her sixth year. She had reached a peak in her career when she died in 1927. She starred in the 1926 revue *The Blackbirds.* After her funeral a flock of blackbirds was released, fluttered over her cortège, and then flew out of sight.

two

THE SHAPE AND SHAPERS OF THE MOVEMENT

The Harlem Renaissance was self-proclaimed and, in the end, it was self-denounced. Alain Locke, who helped to reveal the black talent burgeoning in Harlem by editing *The New Negro* (1925), wrote in 1931: "Has the afflatus of Negro self-expression died down? Are we outliving the Negro fad?"[1] The spiral of literary talent among blacks, then, was brief, but it was an important period in the history of the black American writer. It was an important time for all blacks because it provided the genesis for the search back to a national past. This journey of self-discovery manifested itself variously in the novels and poetry of the Renaissance writers, but the essential element was a questing spirit. That is why some of the black writers of the 1920s—Marita Bonner, Angelina Grimké, and James D. Corrothers, for example—cannot be included among the writers of the Renaissance. The spirit that pervaded the writing of the major and minor writers of the Harlem Renaissance was missing from the works of these writers. There were others who simply ignored the spirit of the times, and some who, after publishing an insignificant poem or story, sensibly gave up writing entirely. A few, notably Arna Bontemps and Zora Neale Hurston, were of the period in time and in spirit but developed and matured artistically later and produced the bulk of their work after the true time of the Harlem Renaissance. In a graphic manner, the Harlem Renaissance might be charted as a smooth curve that begins in 1919, reaches its peak in the years 1925 to 1928, and tapers off in 1932. (A chronology appears in the appendix of this book.)

When Carl Van Vechten's *Nigger Heaven* appeared in 1926, it was merely a link in the chain of events that made the Negro more real to the white world. *Nigger Heaven* helped the Renaissance to get some recognition, but did not—as some would have it—create the movement that made the world see the black man as a creative force in the artistic life of America. Van Vechten, Alain Locke, and James Weldon Johnson formed a spiritual triumvirate dedicated to exposing black artists to the world, and each in his special way was important in nurturing this creative moment in black history. All three men knew one another; Johnson and Van Vechten were especially close friends.

Langston Hughes, who gives a quick but interesting picture of the Renaissance period in his autobiography, *The Big Sea,* presents this view of Alain Locke: "He [Rudolph Fisher] and Alain Locke together were great for intellectual wise-cracking. The two would fling big and witty words about with such swift and punning innuendo that an ordinary mortal just sat and looked wary for fear of being caught in a net of witticisms beyond his cultural ken."[2] Locke, indeed, was a formidable personality on the surface: a graduate of Harvard, the

first black Rhodes Scholar to Oxford, and a student at the
University of Berlin. As an encourager of young black artists,
Locke was supreme. He did not tell them how to write or prod
them to write in one particular mold; he simply encouraged
them to express themselves and gave them advice that was
practical and needed at a time when exposure to the reading
public (mostly white) was difficult for the Negro writer. In a
manner of the spectacular, Alain Locke edited a special edition
of *Survey Graphic* (March 1925) in which the writings of
young Negro artists were exposed to a highly literate and
sophisticated audience. The issue was a smashing success. A
striking portrait by Winold Weiss of the young Roland Hayes
staring dreamily into some unknown world faced the opening
page which announced, quite simply, HARLEM. Alain Locke
went on to explain:

> The Negro today wishes to be known for what he is, even
> in his faults and shortcomings. . . . The pulse of the Negro
> world has begun to beat in Harlem. . . . Our greatest rehab-
> ilitation may possibly come through such channels, but for
> the present, more immediate hope rests in the revaluation
> by white and black alike of the Negro in terms of his artistic
> endowments and cultural contributions, not only in his folk-
> art, music especially, which has always found appreciation,
> but in larger, though humbler and less acknowledged ways. . . .
> A second crop of the Negro's gifts promises still more largely.
> He now becomes a conscious contributor and lays aside the
> status of a beneficiary and ward for that of a collaborator
> and participant in American civilization. The great social
> gain in this is the releasing of our talented group from the
> arid fields of controversy and debate to the productive
> fields of creative expression.[3]

For Locke, then, the path to understanding between the
races might develop as a result of this flowering of talent among

young Negro artists. Some of these writers would soon express
a mild contempt for such a notion, as Langston Hughes did so
splendidly in his now-famous "The Negro Artist and the Racial
Mountain," but Locke was neither chided nor discredited nor
rebuked for intoning this sentiment at a time when presenting
such a special issue was a novelty in itself. Those young black
writers knew the depth of Locke's commitment to the Negro
artist and his art. For instance, Locke was an avid collector of
and writer about African art, and he emphasized the manner
in which these artistic creations proved to white and black
alike "that the Negro is not a cultural foundling without an
inheritance."[4]

Later in 1925, this special issue was expanded and printed
into a book called *The New Negro.* Although Locke continued
to aid and encourage Negro artists, writers, and intellectuals,
for the purpose of understanding his significance in relation
to the Harlem Renaissance one need only read through *The
New Negro* to sense the tremendous role he played. The writers
would have produced their works even without the encouragement of Locke, but with his spiritual and intellectual backing
the movement was given a concrete and meaningful boost.

James Weldon Johnson was quite literally a giant personality
in the black world during the first three decades of the twentieth
century. He was a man who accomplished much in his personal
life, because of the variety of his work, the barriers he over-
came, and the breadth of his interests and involvement in
literature, music, politics, and social justice. He was a significant figure in the Harlem Renaissance, a man whose role was
that of precursor, participant, inspirer, and historian. Johnson
has been called a Renaissance man, and it is significant that
one of the most fruitful periods of his life should have occurred
during the Harlem Renaissance era.

A little over one hundred years ago, on 17 June 1871, James
Weldon Johnson was born in Jacksonville, Florida, of parents

who had spent many years in the British colony of Nassau.
Johnson had a happy childhood, as his reminiscences of his
mother, in particular, reveal: "She belonged to the type of
mothers whose love completely surrounds their children and
is all-pervading; mothers for whom sacrifice for the child means
only an extension of love. . . . The childhood memories that
cluster round my mother are still intensely vivid to me; many
of them are poignantly tender."[5] Both of his parents possessed
exceptional intelligence and culture, although his father was
self-educated. Their combined incomes—Mrs. Johnson was a
teacher, Mr. Johnson a head waiter—provided a healthy enough
income to send Johnson to Atlanta University. He graduated
in 1894 and then went to Stanton School in Jacksonville where
he taught and later became the principal. One of Johnson's
first accomplishments was to study law and to become the
first Negro since Reconstruction to be admitted to the bar in
Florida through open examinations. Johnson turned to the law
after a short-lived side career as editor of a Negro newspaper,
the *Daily American.* His newspaper venture lasted eight months
before he and his partner were forced to suspend publication
because "the colored people of Jacksonville . . . were not able
to support the kind of newspaper I sought to provide for
them."[6] Johnson's next profession, however, brought him
fame and fortune: he collaborated with his brother, J. Rosamond,
and Bob Cole, in the writing of songs for Tin Pan Alley. At one
period in his life, Johnson was still at the Stanton School, practicing law, though not too strenuously, and writing songs in
partnership with his brother and Bob Cole. Johnson gave up
teaching and the law and concentrated on his successful career
in the show business world—a career that ended, while still at
great heights, in 1907. At that time, Johnson, who had been
actively involved in politics, accepted a consular appointment
at Puerto Cabello, Venezuela. He later served as consul at
Corinto, Nicaragua, but left the consular service when Woodrow
Wilson was elected president in 1913.

Important qualities that Johnson shared with Locke and Carl Van Vechten were his ability to perceive talent in young writers and his willingness to aid and encourage them. Johnson, like many of these writers, understood and loved Harlem and felt in the marrow of his bones that this one place was the spiritual and cultural milieu of black Americans. Yet he also saw a certain uniqueness in the temper of life lived by the Negroes in this black metropolis. The "immigrants" to this new land soon shed many of their old ways (or adapted them to city living, as in the case of the rent party) and became New Yorkers. The influence of Harlem was pervasive; a seductive air wafted over its quarters. The Harlem Renaissance writers shared with the ordinary black the realization that this was no ordinary place, no ordinary amalgamation of streets and flats and churches and clubs: here was home. In the words of Claude McKay, each black person, in one sense or another, came "home to Harlem." No one understood this better than Johnson, although he deplored exploitation of Harlem by blacks and whites and cautioned them about it. He wrote a book about Harlem in 1930, *Black Manhattan,* in which he gave a brief description of the Harlem Renaissance as he saw and participated in it.

In *Black Manhattan,* Johnson gives this assessment of the artistic movement in progress:

> The most outstanding phase of the development of the Negro in the United States during the past decade had been the recent literary and artistic emergence of the individual creative artist; and New York has been, almost exclusively, the place where that emergence has taken place. The thing that has happened has been so marked that it does not have the appearance of a development; it seems rather like a sudden awakening, like an instantaneous change.[7]

If anyone understood the Harlem Renaissance, could see it forming, encourage it, analyze it, help to explain it to the world, it was James Weldon Johnson. As both a forerunner and a member of the movement, he presented a living example of the artist-humanist triumphant in a society that sought to disinherit him. He would not be defeated, and he inspired others to feel the same and to express the sentiments of being black in American society.

It was said by many, both black and white, that Carl Van Vechten used Harlem and made a cult of its exotic and more colorfully exciting sections. James Weldon Johnson believed that this was a false view of his friend, and Arna Bontemps agreed with Johnson's judgment of the one white man who literally soaked up black culture during an extensive portion of his life. One of the objections to Van Vechten was his novel, *Nigger Heaven*, published in 1926. Johnson's opinion was that "most of the Negroes who condemned *Nigger Heaven* did not read it; they were estopped by the title."[8] It is a fact, in any case, that Van Vechten did introduce the publishers Alfred and Blanche Knopf to several Negro writers—James Weldon Johnson, for one, and also Rudolph Fisher. According to one of Van Vechten's biographers, "Alfred Knopf often relied on Van Vechten's judgment entirely in decisions about manuscripts [from Negro writers]".[9]

In his time, Van Vechten was famous for his parties where persons of all races met, although at times there were almost more black faces to be seen than white. Despite his own understanding and encouragement of the expression of black culture, Van Vechten still deferred to the judgments of James Weldon Johnson and Rudolph Fisher before publishing *Nigger Heaven*; he wanted to be sure his portrayal of the character traits and the language of blacks (especially the "private Negroese") was true to black life. If one were to put *Nigger Heaven* beside a novel written by a black during the same period, it is doubtful that one would judge it to have been composed by a white man. The novel sounds authentically Negro, even though it is not a particularly good book—not good perhaps for the reasons his biographer happily rattles off: *"Nigger Heaven* is part socio-logical tract, part intellectual history, part aesthetic anthro-pology, but it is all novel."[10]

Even though *Nigger Heaven* fits into the genre of literature for this period in Harlem, the importance of its author goes beyond the book and beyond the age. During the 1920s, Van Vechten helped to bring attention to black artists—writers, performers, and musicians. He brought the white and black worlds together frequently and was a very influential catalyst in the mixed brew of artistry bubbling over in Gotham City. Van Vechten was famous and he was rich. He was a writer, a critic, a photographer, and, by nature, a cosmopolite. His enthusiasm for Harlem and for black life and culture was not the result of a sudden conversion; he had been interested in blacks since his early life, and he developed this even further when, as a college student, he attended performances by Negro musicians and singers. But his "addiction," as he himself termed it, for the darker citizens of the United States grew more pro-nounced in the early 1920s. Van Vechten was a serious gadabout in the clubs, theatres, shops, and homes of Harlem. He savored every moment he spent in what was, for most whites, a purlieu not only of Manhattan but of civilization itself. Van Vechten, however, didn't stop with going to Harlem: he also brought Harlem to his elegant home in mid-Manhattan:

> After his marriage to the Russian actress, Fania Marinoff, he developed his own fabulous reputation as a genial, imagina-tive host drawing to the Van Vechten apartments the high and the low, the exotic and the plain, the dark and the light, the intellectual and the emotional representatives of litera-ture, society, and the arts. All together, his social exploits qualify him as a ringmaster worthy of star billing in the Circus Maximus of the Twenties.[11]

Part of the Van Vechten charm was his unabashed enthusi-asm for the new and the interesting. He judged each person, each act, each artistic production on its own merits. His interest in Walter White's novel, *Fire in the Flint* (1924), led him to contact the author; years later, Van Vechten reminisced, " 'Walter and I got on like a house afire.' "[12] It was the beginning of a deeper immersion into black life and the black world that spread like black ink from 110th Street northward, away from the chic midtown towers where the Van Vechtens lived. Even though the Harlem Renaissance was forming and rising at this time, even though it would have become a reality without Carl Van Vechten, it owes a debt to him for popularizing and supporting it. Without white support the Harlem Renaissance would have suffered from a lack of money and readers, and Carl Van Vechten was a prime mover in securing this patronage.

There is a note to Carl Van Vechten from Countee Cullen in the Cullen file at Yale in which the poet briefly discusses the donation of an original manuscript to Van Vechten. To establish a collection of Negro literature at the Yale University Library had been a dream of Van Vechten's since the late 1940s. Through gifts of his writer friends and others, through gifts of his own (including some of his justifiably highly praised photographs), Van Vechten was finally able to realize his dream when the James Weldon Johnson Memorial Collection of Negro Arts and Letters was dedicated officially on 7 January 1950. This contribution to the black arts is enough to enshrine the name of Carl Van Vechten as one of those who valued the black man's contribution to America's artistic tradition.

There were many others who championed the writers of the Harlem Renaissance—Fannie Hurst, Zona Gale, and Jessie Fauset, for instance—but two men, in particular, should be mentioned: W. E. B. DuBois and Charles S. Johnson.

DuBois's relationship to the Harlem Renaissance is a bit curious and distant. He abhorred the portrayals of low life, such as in the novels of Claude McKay, yet he recognized the genuine talent of Langston Hughes. The concern, however, that formed the nexus between this thorough New Englander and the new men of the Harlem Renaissance was "the race." Racial pride was forceful in DuBois; it was the sort of pride that had faith in at least a portion of the black race. He called upon the "talented tenth," of whom the writers were a part, to show to the world the Negro's beauty and strength. The fear DuBois voiced from time to time was a fear that the black writer would forget his duty to uplift the race and to elevate the rest of the world's opinion about his black brethren. In his review of *The New Negro* DuBois wrote:

> If Mr. Locke's thesis is insisted on too much it is going to turn the Negro renaissance into decadence. It is the fight for Life and Liberty that is giving birth to Negro literature and art today and when, turning from this fight or ignoring it, the young Negro tries to do pretty things or things that catch the passing fancy of the really unimportant critics and publishers about him, he will find that he has killed the soul of Beauty in his Art.[13]

The interest DuBois had in the movement was not ignored—indeed, as the editor-in-chief of *The Crisis* he was an obvious influence—but it was one that remained on an intellectual rather than a personal plane. In his articles and various discussions, he attempted to define and, through definition, to direct the unifying elements in this whole artistic movement. DuBois's main weakness was his inability to realize that his predilection for propagandizing for the race through art was a flaw that all the rhetoric in the world could not cure.

Charles S. Johnson is not as well known as DuBois, Locke, or James Weldon Johnson but is, nevertheless, praised by Langston Hughes as one who "did more to encourage and develop Negro writers during the 1920's than anyone else in

America."[14] Johnson was a sociologist, the first black president of Fisk University, and also the editor of *Opportunity* for five and a half years. Johnson's initiation of the *Opportunity* contests gave the reading public and literary critics exposure to a variety of talented Negro writers, such as Hughes, Arthur H. Fauset, John Matheus, and Bontemps, and gave much-needed encouragement (and some money) to the young writers. Recently it has been noted that

> it was in the *Opportunity* contests and dinners, however, that Charles S. Johnson was most successful as an entrepreneur in promoting the new awakening of black culture. Johnson recognized the creative genius of the many black artists of the 1920's. But this genius was of limited value until the racial barriers of publishers were removed. Johnson, along with Urban League official William H. Baldwin, moved deliberately to bring the white publishers and the black writers together.[15]

It is in this context, then, that Charles S. Johnson effected his greatest influence upon the fledgling black writers of this period. His intelligence, his selflessness in the cause of these beginning artists, and his ceaseless encouragement of them in practical, remunerative manners earn him a high place among the primary patrons of Harlem Renaissance writers.

By 1924 there was little question that a movement was stirring. *Cane,* the most remarkable piece of literature to emerge from the Harlem Renaissance, had been published during the previous year; poets like Countee Cullen, Langston Hughes, and Claude McKay were mentioned with frequency and with praise. This rash of folk expression, touching upon the very nature of the black soul, strengthened and matured quickly during the quixotic twenties, shaping itself and growing, in part, through the encouragement of these deans of black intellectual life in America. Locke and DuBois believed keenly in the idea of the "talented tenth"; James Weldon Johnson, in his own way, also believed that a demonstration of intellectual stamina and talent among Negro creators would change the world's view of the black man. Carl Van Vechten recognized a spawning of talent that could not be denied and should not go unrewarded, and he aided in basically practical ways. Van Vechten also helped to advance the cause of the black artist by his genuine acceptance of the contribution of blacks to American arts and letters. Last, in his role as a real friend to the Negro, Van Vechten was able to bring about what DuBois and James Weldon Johnson had lamented seldom occurred— social, cultural, and intellectual intercourse between the leaders, the "aristocracy," of both races.

From 1924 until the end, or at least the ebb of the movement, there was a series of hosannas and praise and benediction. The few shrill cries of dissent were vociferously countered by more paeans from the literary gods. There was an exhilaration that was captured in many earnest efforts. Although individual works often suffered under close critical scrutiny, praise was routinely given to some part of nearly every work penned by a black author. The works which were produced attempted to dramatize the resentment the black man held against racial prejudice or the illogical or foolish aspects of such prejudice. Of course, there were the folksy and the bizarre and the exotic tales. Finally, whatever the special quality of a particular offering, there was always the pride of race, the search for roots, the belief that black writers and artists possessed sparks of genius that would set the nation aflame.

NOTES

1. Alain Locke, "This Year of Grace," *Opportunity* 9 (February 1931): 48.

2. Langston Hughes, *The Big Sea* (New York: Hill and Wang, 1940), pp. 240-241.

3. *Survey Graphic* 53 (March 1925): 632, 633, 634.

4. Ibid., 673.

5. James Weldon Johnson, *Along This Way* (New York: Viking, 1933), p. 11.

6. Ibid., p. 140.

7. James Weldon Johnson, *Black Manhattan* (New York: Knopf, 1940, c. 1930), p. 260.

8. Johnson, *Along This Way*, p. 382.

9. Edward Lueders, *Carl Van Vechten and the Twenties* (Albuquerque: University of New Mexico Press, 1955), p. 65.

10. Ibid., p. 87.

11. Ibid., p. 24.

12. Bruce Kellner, *Carl Van Vechten and the Irreverent Decades* (Norman: University of Oklahoma Press, 1968), p. 197.

13. *The Crisis* 31 (1926): 141.

14. Hughes, *The Big Sea*, p. 218.

15. Patrick J. Gilpin, "Charles S. Johnson: Entrepreneur of the Harlem Renaissance." In Arna Bontemps, editor, *The Harlem Renaissance Remembered* (New York: Dodd, 1972), p. 224.

three

TWO OUTCASTS

Claude McKay spent his time abroad during the height of the Harlem Renaissance, and Jean Toomer mentally, spiritually, and physically had left the movement by 1925. Yet their influence on the Renaissance was pervasive and they hovered spiritually over the other writers. Both suffered a measure of rejection, real or imagined, by their fellow black artists. There was the reserve and radicalism of McKay, non-American, British-educated proud of his blackness, and often homesick for the soft, balmy land of his birth. And Toomer, the enigma, as restless as McKay and spiritually confused as well, tried to fashion a philosophy of racelessness after composing the work that would forever give him a place in black American literature. These two vagabonds (in a measure, outcasts) straddled the decade, McKay producing much, Toomer publishing little. It is not entirely surprising that each chose an identifiable religious concept by which to live out the end of his days.

McKay epitomized what many black authors strove to discover: the poet and prosodist as black writer—black in tone, in pose, in idiom—a being who was unique yet not odd. McKay, like Langston Hughes, found his black self in writing; but McKay, curiously enough, finally dichotomized his writing into black prose and standard English poetry. Still, McKay had no major identity crisis as a black man and wrote without any apparent strain or self-consciousness. His primary problem seemed to be rootlessness, the spirit of the restless vagabond who found relief only late in life when he was converted to Catholicism.

There was one issue on which McKay spoke out vehemently: assimilation of the black into the white culture. He shared Garvey's disdain for what he considered the black American's exaggerated desire for integration. He expressed his views of Afro-Americans by writing: "It [the Negro race] sadly lacks a group soul. And the greatest hindrance to the growth of a group soul is the wrong idea held about segregation. Negroes do not understand the differences between group segregation and group aggregation."[1]

The work of Claude McKay reveals itself in stages, first in poetry, later in prose. His first two books, *Songs of Jamaica*, published in Kingston, Jamaica, in 1912, and *Constab Ballads*, published in London in 1912, reflect his early life and are often written in Jamaican dialect. Later in his life, McKay inscribed a copy of *Constab Ballads* with the note that it was "my one book I should like to be destroyed."[2] These two books, however, were merely prefatory to his more important (from the Harlem Renaissance point of view) collection of poetry, *Harlem Shadows*, which appeared in 1922. (This had been published, minus some of the poems in the 1922 edition, in England in 1920 under the title *Spring in New Hampshire and Other Poems*.) Here the power of McKay as poet is apparent. In this work we are introduced to the themes (e.g., nostalgia for Jamaica and alienation) that preoccupied McKay throughout the important phases of his literary career.

McKay's personal and literary leanings were largely influenced
by Jamaica, where he was born in 1889. His birthdate hints
that he will be in certain respects different from many of the
other Harlem Renaissance writers. McKay had received recognition in England and Jamaica as a poet by the time he arrived
in the United States in 1912; hence, it is little wonder that the
restraints of a bourgeois black college such as Tuskegee Institute,
where he studied agriculture for a few months, helped to dis-
illusion him about the American Negro. At this time also McKay
was introduced to that special brand of American racism found
in the Southern states then. The shock to his sensitive soul was
irreparable although he decided to purge himself of the hatred
blacks can feel against whites. After studying agricultural
science at Kansas State College, McKay went to New York
where he "was determined to find expression in writing."[3]
Only after five years of writing and working at a variety of
menial jobs did he receive any recognition as a poet in the
United States. In 1918 McKay met Frank Harris of *Pearson's
Magazine* and soon afterward met and commenced a lifelong
friendship with Max Eastman and his sister, Crystal. This was
the beginning, too, of McKay's identification with radical thinkers
of the day, and a subsequent journey to the Soviet Union
served to strengthen the notion that McKay was a Marxist and
a radical. He was probably never a true Marxist (he was berated
in the 1930s for what was considered an abandonment of
Marxist beliefs), but anyone with McKay's passionate concern
for justice for the black man probably was radical.[4]

It is interesting that McKay employed the most traditional
forms of poetic expression, the sonnet and other rhymed verse
in iambic pentameter. There are vigor and passion in his poetry;
there is also tenderness of the most romantic sort. His themes
were remarkably consistent and they were reasserted later in
his novels and short stories. There was, first of all, the theme
stemming from his being a black man—a bitter denunciation
of racial prejudice. The most famous example of this theme is
the poem, "If We Must Die," written in 1919 as a memorial
to the race riots and revived in 1939 by Winston Churchill be-

cause of its stirring cry for men not to go to their death without a fight:

> O let us nobly die,
> So that our precious blood may not be shed
> In vain; then even the monsters we defy
> Shall be constrained to honor us though dead!

McKay's nostalgia for Jamaica was exhibited in those poems celebrating the freer life, one that is close to the earth and sky and water. This reverence for nature reveals the poet's longing for religion (nature, at first, is his religion). His subsequent conversion to Catholicism was not as uncharacteristic as some would have it. Even the symbols he used in his nature poetry point toward a preoccupation not only with antimetropolis sentiments but also with man's religious dependency. His choice of language frequently demonstrates this: "In benediction over nun-like hills" ("Tropics in New York"), "And some called it the resurrection flower" ("The Easter Flower"), and "Even the sacred moments when we played,/ All innocent of passion, uncorrupt" ("Flame-Heart").

The theme of alienation is iterated in McKay's poetry (but is most vividly expressed through Ray, a character in two of his novels and ostensively the spokesman for McKay). This strong sense of alienation is expressed on two levels: black in the white world (or black against white and vice versa), and black against black. The latter theme is almost exclusively portrayed in his novels; the former emotion is expressed in many poems, such as "Outcast," "Baptism," "Courage," and "America." McKay's vagabond life was the actual playing out of the alienation he proclaims in his poetry; for, as the last two lines of "Outcast" declare, he felt keenly in his youth that

> I was born, far from my native clime,
> Under a white man's menace, out of time.[5]

Even the turn to Catholicism could not completely eradicate
this sentiment, although by that time (1942) McKay had completed all of his important writings.

McKay was always fascinated by the black man's vitality
and the richness of his innate creativity, his joy in living despite
oppression, and the authenticity of an irrepressible strength
deriving from his primitive heritage. Many critics, especially
blacks, scolded McKay for his apparent acquiescence in the
cult of the primitive and his penchant for portraying the natural-
istic black man as a savage in society. While McKay did not feel
that he was exploiting his race, he did believe that the black
man had his own special vitality and grace. These notions are
clearly seen in such poems as "Alfonso, Dressing to Wait at
Table," "Outcast," and "Harlem Dancer." The sensuousness
that pervades most of his poetry points more subtly to this
motif, although the line between lyrical emotionalism and
sensualism may be fine or even indistinguishable.

It was said of Countee Cullen that he suffered from a "taint
of artiness";[6] the same might be said of McKay's poetry. Because of his British background and his upbringing in the literature of the Anglo-Saxon world, McKay does show the restraints
characteristic of the European tradition. (According to Max
Eastman's biographical note in *Selected Poems of Claude McKay*,
the poet was called the "Jamaican Bobbie Burns.") McKay did
not use poetry to its fullest power to express the concerns most
important to him as a literary artist. Another of his weaknesses
was inherent in his restless romantic nature: trite or weak expressions and threadbare phrases, such as "ghostly white," "river's
breast," "earth's white breast," "soft like the dew," or "earth's
vast womb." This lack of a more complex mode of expression,
this attenuation of his vocabulary, combined with his power-
lessness to pull away from traditional verse forms to proclaim
the unique quality of blackness, are two weaknesses he never
remedied. In addition, his belief that social and aesthetic sentiments should not be wedded in poetry formed a self-imposed
limitation. It will be noted later that he followed no such philosophy in his novels.

The critic who was offended by Claude McKay's novels had glowing praise for Jean Toomer:

> Finally in Jean Toomer we come upon the very first artist of the race, who with all an artist's passion and sympathy for life, its hurts, its sympathies, its desires, its joy, its defeats and strange yearnings, can write about the Negro without the surrender or compromise of the artist's vision. *Cane* is a book of gold and bronze, of dusk and flame, of ecstasy and pain, and Jean Toomer is a bright morning star of a new day of the race in literature.[7]

This was rather strong acclaim from the proper Bostonian William Braithwaite. Yet he was not the only critic to heap encomiums upon that enigmatic figure, Jean Toomer, who provided the Harlem Renaissance with its most experimental and most individualistic literary production, *Cane.*

Toomer was a mulatto who was as pale as any white man, and it is never forgotten that he twice married white women and spent his last forty-odd years in a predominantly white world. From the artistic point of view, this hardly matters, for he relinquished the life of the serious writer, as far as one can now surmise, some time during the mid-1930s.[8] His views on race and its meaning are important because his primary concept might explain, in part, his disavowal of the literary life.

Toomer's background sheds a certain amount of light on his development as a writer, not only in racial terms but also in terms of environment. He was born in Washington, D.C., in 1894, of Creole parents whose antecedents harked back to P. B. S. Pinchback, acting governor of Louisiana during the Reconstruction. Toomer once denied the fact that Pinchback had black ancestry, and this was interpreted as a repudiation of his black blood. This denial was probably a part of his groping toward a philosophy of racelessness which he finally declared in 1930. Toomer attended the University of Wisconsin from 1914 to 1915 where he studied agriculture. He then taught school in Sparta, Georgia, for four months, after which he

traveled and worked at various jobs. Later he delved into mysticism, embarking on a spiritual venture which culminated in a
few summers spent at the Gurdjieff Institute in Fontainebleau.
He first went there in 1924 to study Georges Ivanovitch
Gurdjieff's system of attaining "new levels of experience,
beginning with the difficult first step to self-consciousness
and progressing to world- and possibly cosmic-consciousness."[9]
Toomer came back to the United States and held some discussion
sessions in which he attempted to proselytize some of his acquaintances and friends.[10] Later he turned to the Quakers and
remained among them until his death in 1967. It was a strange
end for the genius of the Harlem Renaissance.

More than any other black writer of that time, Toomer
enunciated the themes of prose and poetry that dominated
the work of the lost generation writers: modern man's spiritual
dearth, obsession with death, rejection of bourgeois values,
loss of identity (contrasted with a search for one)—in other
words, the theme of man in an "age of anxiety." On the other
hand, he shared with his black brothers a pride in race, a belief
in the black man's vitality, a recognition of a certain sterility
in white life, a feeling that white conventions would taint black
culture, and, perhaps most important, a search for the black
man's roots in the past. As Robert A. Bone has pointed out,
the figure of Father John in the "Kabnis" section of *Cane*
emphasizes Toomer's concern for this "link with the Negro's
ancestral past."[11] This is vividly apparent in the story of
"Carma" when, for instance, Toomer ascribes to the dusty
Dixie Pike the power to join with a goat path in Africa.

Toomer, indeed, appears to have seen life as a continuous
flow of movement from one condition to another, a continuum
that has variations in different "rites of passage." The Afro-
American's early life, the ancestral period, is the beginning of
a movement through phases of life that are finally incorporated
into the American society, for good or bad. Still there is flux:
the territorial separation from Africa must be bridged by an
acknowledgment of the African past and a formulation of a
philosophy that links the black American with the black

African. The best example of this is seen in the concluding
section of "Kabnis" in which the language and action serve
each other conjunctively as Kabnis recommences his life with
a sort of new birth.

Portions of *Cane* appeared in magazines *(Broom, The Crisis,*
the *Prairie Schooner* were three), and one section was printed
in the 1923 edition of *The Best Short Stories of the Year.*
Although he published other pieces of fiction and poetry,
Cane was his masterpiece. Actually, it is the single collection
of his writings, for *Aphorisms* (1931) is an anomalous collection
of his work. *Aphorisms* expresses Toomer's philosophy in a
transitional period of his life and, therefore, may provide a key
to what Toomer, the man (as opposed to the artist), became.

Critics will argue over whether *Cane* is a novel because the
book contains poetry both within and following the central
stories. As Arna Bontemps has reminded us: "Reviewers who
read it in 1923 were generally stumped. Poetry and prose were
whipped together in a kind of frappé."[12] One can, of course,
get around the problem by calling the book poetry, or poetic
prose, and then refer to Toomer's admiration of Whitman and
his preoccupation with religion and mysticism. It is no wonder
that poetry and prose were woven throughout the book, for
Toomer was writing about life and life is not consistently one
thing or another. The problems of existence that Toomer explored were realistic enough. The style in which he chose to
reveal them was impressionistic or, as one critic suggested,
"exhibits a totally liberated language and one which commands
the nightmare sharpness and displacement of imagery that characterize surrealist art."[13]

Cane is divided into three sections, a fact that suggests triadic
symbolism. The middle portion, set in Washington, D.C., and
Chicago, serves as a bridge for and contrast to the other two
sections that are laid in Georgia. All of his characters, regardless of geographic location, are affected by their own personal
isolation and fallibility. It is a black-white world beset by the
sort of normal-abnormal madness that Anderson described in
Winesberg, Ohio.

In the first section, Toomer seems obsessed by his female characters. This part of the book has warmth, sensuousness, and vibrancy; yet there are stagnation and passivity as well. The passion that seethes through the lives of the characters and permeates the six stories illustrates Toomer's remarkable control of tone. The first story, "Karintha," is brief but pulsating; the recurrent symbols of the hobby-horse, the setting sun, and the sawdust pile from the sawmill establish Toomer's preoccupation with life and death. Karintha is that beauty ripened too soon, "Karintha carrying beauty, perfect as dusk when the sun goes down."[14] She gives her body to men who do not understand that her early physical maturity was to be her doom. She has a child who "fell out of her womb onto a bed of pine-needles," and the child is committed to the pile of sawdust (phallic) which is burning and sending up smoke that "spreads itself out over the valley" (as Karintha has done with her body). Henceforth, Karintha gives her body for money; her life, like the dusk (like her skin, too) is deficient of light, and she lives a bit on the brink of the world, "on the eastern horizon/When the sun goes down./Goes down" (5).

In this first story, the reader is introduced to Toomer's use of the wind, a life-moving force as opposed to stagnancy. Closely related to this is the focus upon the four elements—earth, air, fire, and water—that function as symbols of life and death. Fire, for instance, has a double meaning; for Karintha's child dies upon the sawdust pile (fire), but the smoke from this fire rises to take the (saved) child's soul to Jesus. Then there is the repeated use of the word "dusk." In a later story, "Fern," he writes of the dusk: "Dusk, suggesting the almost imperceptible procession of giant trees, settled with a purple haze about the cane. I felt strange, as I always do in Georgia, particularly at dusk. I felt that things unseen to men were tangibly immediate" (31). There may be, then, two levels of usage for this symbol—obscurity and its opposite, insight.

The best story from this section, "Esther," illustrates Toomer's portrayal of failures in life, people who are afraid of living out the deep stirrings within themselves, stirrings that have been strengthened by dreams. Esther, like other Toomer characters, cannot come to grips with reality. She is also one of several of his characters who represent, as Robert Bone quite rightly insists, "a series of burial or confinement symbols."[15] Toomer takes us through four stages of Esther's life: at nine, she encounters King Barlo for the first time; at sixteen, she dreams of conceiving and bearing King Barlo's child; at twenty-two, she "thinks about men" (42) and thinks about Barlo and decides that she loves him; at twenty-seven she offers herself to King Barlo. Toomer thus presents an obsession that grows from a repressed spirit. Esther is the light-skinned daughter of the richest Negro in town; thus, both her color and her position isolate her. At the end of the story, her isolation, following the shame she brings upon herself (also the one positive act towards life that she performs), is complete and she falls back into her sterile, deathlike life. This end has been prefigured in the opening portion of the story in which we see Esther, "her cheeks too flat and dead . . . like a little white child, starched, frilled" (36). The image is of someone lifeless, as if she were actually dead and about to be placed on a funeral bier. Then she espies King Barlo, the personification of life, a vital, muscular man, the "Black buck archetype."[16] These two represent opposites at all levels of contrasts and iterate Toomer's concern with life and death, the black man's essential vitality, and the sterile lives of many of those who bear the taint of miscegenation.

Esther's eventual movement towards King Barlo, she thinks, is to save him. Yet, isn't it her own salvation she is seeking through King Barlo, savior (the father) and dream-lover? She at first represses her sexual desire for him and then gives in to it alternately as she hurries towards Nat Bowle's place. When she is before King Barlo she is repelled: "The thought comes suddenly, that conception with a drunken man must be a mighty sin" (48). She returns to her original self—virginal,

unmoved, stagnant, as if "there is no air, no street, and the
town has completely disappeared" (48). She has saved herself
from sin (i.e., hell) because she cannot face real life. In a way,
she has placed herself in another hell—the hell of a quotidian
existence that is incremental only in measurable time: year
upon year will come, but Esther will experience nothing beyond
the moment of her retreat from King Barlo.

In the second section, Esther has her counterpart in the
character of Muriel in the sketch, "Box Seat." Here the confinement motif underpins the portrayal of one woman's inability
to surrender to the man who is drawn to her and who attracts
her. The language points to Muriel's circumscribed world: "iron
gate," "bolt," "musselhead" (a description that Dan Moore,
Muriel's lover, gives to her watchful landlady), "break in," "zoo
restrictions," "keeper-taboos," "the house contracts about him"
(107); "the house, the rows of houses locked about her chair"
(113); "the rap is like cool thick glass between them, Dan and
Muriel cannot breach the chasm that separates them: his world
is one of feeling and warm passion, hers is one of coolness, a
prim, lifeless world. When, at the end, she is forced to accept the
bloodstained white flower, her momentary act of embracing
the real and vibrant world precipitates Dan to jump up and
shout his equivocal pronouncement: "JESUS WAS ONCE A
LEPER!" (129). Dan now exchanges character with Muriel,
for he becomes "as cool as a green stem that has just shed its
flower" (129). He is freed of his passion, but ironically his
personality becomes like Muriel's, passionless and cool. The
last image, that of Dan walking down the street, forgetful of
the man he is to fight, could mean that Dan has, indeed, per-
manently changed, has become, as Bone suggests, a sterile
man. [17] The world around Dan is full of smells and black
vibrancy, offering the possibility that he will reenter this world
after he is completely rid of his passion for Muriel. After all,
"I am Dan Moore. I was born in a canefield. The hands of
Jesus touched me. I am come to a sick world to heal it" (105-

106). Is this to say that Dan is a Christ-figure? If so, how does
this connect with his sexual love for Muriel? The serene Dan
at the end shows indifference, not a Christlike compassion or
interest in his fellowman. The author has left room for specula-
tion. In the last section of *Cane*, however, Toomer appears to
bind up his ending a bit more clearly.

The "Kabnis" section of *Cane* richly elaborates some of
Toomer's major concerns. Ralph Kabnis is the intellectual,
the sensitive young man in the hostile world that he alternately
hates and loves. At one moment, awed by the night's beauty,
he falls to his knees in a supplicant's pose that prefigures his
subsequent conversion and rebirth. Georgia will be the place
of his trial and agony and his search for self, for Ralph is a
man in search of soul—the ultimate soul, and the soul of blackness. For Kabnis, they may be one and the same.

"Kabnis" is divided into six sections; each one is a movement
toward the salvation of Kabnis. He acts out his life in a series of
tableaux in which he alternately seeks and rejects knowledge
of himself and the world. Throughout the story, Toomer has
used earth, air, wind, and fire to symbolize the body and spirit
advancing toward personal salvation. Wind and fire are the
strongest symbols. The apocalyptic old man is rebaptized
Father John, thus paralleling him with St. John: "A mute
John the Baptist of a new religion—or a tongue-tied shadow
of an old" (211). In the end, it is this old man and the innocent
young girl, Carrie, who accomplish the conversion of the once-
blind Kabnis.

Section I introduces the reader to Kabnis, a young, intense
man who is trying to pull himself together and come to terms
with reality. He is a teacher in a Georgia school, and he finds
it nearly impossible to accept the smug respectability that
schools of this sort espouse. The wind is introduced immediately: "Night winds in Georgia are vagrant poets, whispering.
Kabnis, against his will, lets his book slip down, and listens to
them" (157). Kabnis, who wants to reject what the wind sym-

bolizes—life and the gifts of the Holy Spirit—listens against his
will and therefore moves imperceptively closer to salvation.[18]

Kabnis slips softly into a dreamworld where he wishes to
change himself from a weakling into a strong, aggressive man.
A rat scampers across the room and shakes him out of his
dream. He utters a vague premonition of a change that might
come about: "Something as sure as fate was going to happen"
(159). The following episode with the chicken, in which he
kills it and gets blood upon his hands, contrasts with the scene
that follows: Kabnis, fists heavenward, then, suddenly, upon
his knees. This moment, just one prefiguration of his conversion, epitomizes the unnatural tension that the black person
and the black artist feel in a constricted society. Twice, near
the end of this first section, Ralph reiterates his self-admonition—
"Ralph, pull yourself together" (162)—and this quasi-leitmotif
strengthens the notion that the story will move towards some
act that will permit him to do this. The wind is the last sound
in this section.

Section II brings the reader to Sunday, at the home of Fred
Halsey, the reasonable man, the man who personifies dignity
through labor; he is one who has come to terms with life. He
has accomplished this by accepting his position as a black man
in Southern society; thus, he is still at the mercy of the white
man and has a taint of "spiritual degradation" and moral
inertia.[19] Even so, he will perform his part in aiding Ralph to
rehabilitate himself. Certainly Halsey is more of a help to the
young man than Layman, the other character in this scene.
There is subtle irony in naming the preacher-teacher Layman,
for this seems to spell out what becomes apparent later in the
scene: that his power as a man of God is not particularly useful;
that, despite his profession, he is not endowed with special
powers that might set him apart from any member of his congregation. Only a man like Lewis, a visionary, a mystic, a man
who acts according to his beliefs, can offer relief to a seeker

like Ralph. Lewis seems to be both a Christ-figure and a mani-
festation of the other side of Ralph's psyche.

A contrapuntal tension is built up between the expression
of self-doubt on the part of Kabnis and the sounds of spiritual
singing emanating from the church next door. This self-doubt,
combined with a fear of being in the South, is also played off
against the story of Mame Lamkins whose child was ripped
from her womb and then nailed to a tree. This story serves not
only to heighten the fear within Kabnis but also to form a
contrast between the North and the South. The South, despite
its nurtured savagery, will become the place where Ralph Kabnis
will discover his racial roots. This is an irony of contrasts, for
the "free" North cannot provide what the deprived South can
and will offer to Kabnis, namely, self-renewal, both spiritual
and racial. Kabnis's flight at the end of this chapter is consistent
with his unformed, spiritually stagnant character.

In the third section of this story, Kabnis's life moves to a
crisis point, and a broad hint of his conversion is given during
his confrontation with Lewis. The author's description of the
encounter reveals the need for both men to connect with each
other. But Kabnis is still too weak to face up to his fate:

> His [Lewis's] eyes turn to Kabnis. In the instant of their
> shifting, a vision of the life they are to meet. Kabnis, a prom-
> ise of a soil-soaked beauty; uprooted, thinning out. Suspended
> a few feet above the soil whose touch would resurrect him. . . .
> There is a swift interchange of consciousness. Kabnis has a
> sudden need to rush into the arms of this man . . . then a
> savage, cynical twist-about within mocks his impulse and
> strengthens him to replace Lewis (191, 192).

At the conclusion, it is to Halsey that Kabnis submits. He goes
with Halsey to work at his shop and thus changes the course
of his life both physically and spiritually.

It is in this segment also that the reader is presented with
what was to become a type of villain in black literature—the
accomodator, the sycophant, the "Negro who thinks there is

no one quite so suave and polished as himself" (185). He is
Professor Hanby, the head of the school where Kabnis works,
and it is he who lives "to prove to the world that the Negro
race can be just like any other race" (186). He means, of course,
that blacks ought to try being just like whites. When he dis-
misses Kabnis, he releases the young man from the false academic world that blacks like Hanby have fashioned. This act
represents for Kabnis another step into the true racial past.

Halsey's workshop in section IV is the place of Kabnis's
spiritual apprenticeship in addition to being a place to learn
a new trade for sustaining himself. Just as he "is awkward and
ludicrous, like a schoolboy in his big brother's new overalls"
(196) while at work, his state of mind is also maladroit and a
bit absurd. Carrie K., the sister of Fred Halsey, is introduced;
her presence brings a touch of innocence and joy into the book.
She has not yet been ruined by the South or by experience;
even so, she is an integral part of that land and of her family—
a family that also now includes Kabnis.

As the story moves into section V, a sensuous note is sounded;
and, indeed, it is here that Halsey and Kabnis perform the
physical act of love in the presence of the old man who will
rehabilitate Kabnis to the spiritual act of love. The old man,
who is sinless, ignores the sexual acts because they are ultimately
insignificant. It is a coming-into-self, through connecting with
the past, that will be the consequential act.

After Lewis has renamed the old man Father John, Toomer
appears to have shifted the burden of Kabnis's salvation to the
older man. The frenzied evening forces Lewis into a retreat,
but not before he says to Kabnis: "Cant hold them, can you?
Master; slave. Soil; the overarching heavens. Dusk; dawn. They
fight and bastardize you" (218). He has served his function
and has no more of himself to give.

In the last section, Kabnis is finally left alone with the old
man. Kabnis has fallen and faints away under the impact of
his fall. As he rises about an hour later, "light of a new sun is

about to filter through the windows" (230). A light will soon filter through Kabnis's soul. Kabnis tries to dismiss the old man and his significance, but the coming of Carrie K. subdues him. He then asks her, "An how would you help me, child, dear sweet sister?" (234). This submissive remark plays into the pattern of his salvation, for he now admits that "its th soul of me that needs th risin" (234). Still, he is not quite prepared for his new way of life. Father John must speak. It is a shock and a revelation to hear Father John affix sin upon the white race—"O th sin th white folks 'mitted when they made th Bible lie" (237)—and he is nearly unable to sustain the significance of such an utterance. But Carrie K. helps him; she and Lewis and Father John form a triune working for Kabnis's salvation. It is the tableau of Carrie and Father John, along with the rising sun, which imprints the strong sense that Kabnis's trudge upward is both a spiritual rebirth and an acknowledgment of his link to the racial heritage of the black race: "The sun arises. Gold-glowing child, it steps into the sky and sends a birth-song slanting down gray dust streets and sleepy windows of the southern town" (239).

The language and symbols in this portion of *Cane* are rich. Toomer uses metaphors effectively (e.g., "Night winds in Georgia are vagrant poets"), and has an arresting array of symbols, both human (e.g., Layman), material (e.g., towers, windows), and elemental (e.g., the half-moon, the sun, the wind). His unpunctuated contractions (*cant, thats, dont*), suppressed endings (*th, risin, spinnin*), word conjoinings (*moren* ["more than"], *theres* ["there is"—this is not a contraction]), dialect spellings (*yassur, fer, seed* ["seen"], *sholy* ["surely"]), and Georgia dialect itself (*atreein, ahackin, faller, usall*) reinforce both the themes and tone of the sketch. Toomer's language thus achieves the effect of music, a certain lyricism that either replicates or creates an authentic folkloric quality of rural Georgia during the early part of the twentieth century.

Finally, the thematic assertion of the racial past as meaningful for the living present is all-pervasive in "Kabnis." Toomer

wrote to the editors of the *Liberator* about Georgia's influence
on him: "A visit to Georgia last fall was the starting point of
almost everything of worth that I have done. I heard folk-songs
come from the lips of Negro peasants. I saw the rich dusk beauty
that I had heard many false accents about, and of which till
then, I was somewhat skeptical. And a deep part of my nature,
a part that I had repressed, sprang suddenly to life and responded
to them."[20]

Toomer's subsequent defection from "the race" into the
world at large ("I am of no particular race. I am of the human
race") in no way detracts from the enormous importance of
Cane. As Arthur P. Davis has observed: "No white man could
have written this work. Perhaps no Negro who had to spend all
of his life in Georgia could have written it. Because of his dual
background (North and South) and his status as a 'volunteer
Negro,' Toomer could walk and *feel* on both sides of the racial
street. It is this combination that accounts in part for *Cane*'s
excellence."[21] Certainly it is a work of art that invites constant
examination; Toomer's use of the dream, his symbols, the
poetry, and Biblical and mythical parallels are some aspects
that need repeated scrutiny. In this way, we would deepen
our understanding of the most complex personality of the
Harlem Renaissance.

NOTES

1. Claude McKay, *A Long Way From Home* (New York: Lee Furman,
1937), p. 350.

2. The copy of this book is at the Beinecke Library (Yale University).

3. McKay, *A Long Way From Home*, p. 4.

4. In his autobiography, *A Long Way From Home*, McKay wrote:
"I could never be a disciplined member of any Communist party, for I
was born to be a poet" (p. 173).

5. Claude McKay, *Selected Poems of Claude McKay* (New York:
Bookman Associates, 1953), p. 41.

6. *Atlantic Monthly* 179 (March 1947): 145.

7. William Stanley Braithwaite, "The Negro in American Literature."
In Addison Gayle, Jr., editor, *Black Expression* (New York: Weybright
and Tally, 1969), p. 181.

8. Fisk University now has Toomer's papers, and subsequent publications will indicate how late into life Toomer pursued literature. A section from Toomer's unpublished biography, *Earth-being* (*Black Scholar,* January 1971) is dated ca. 1927-1934.

9. Jean Toomer, *Cane* (New York: Harper and Row, 1969, c. 1923), p. xiii.

10. Statement made to author by Arna Bontemps in a taped interview at Yale University, 18 December 1970.

11. Robert A. Bone, *The Negro Novel in America,* revised edition (New Haven: Yale, 1965), p. 88.

12. Toomer, *Cane,* p. x.

13. Gerald Moore, "Poetry in the Harlem Renaissance." In C. W. E. Bigsby, editor, *The Black American Writer,* vol. 2 (Baltimore: Penguin Books, 1969), p. 72.

14. Toomer, *Cane,* p. 5. All subsequent quotes will have page numbers indicated within the text.

15. Bone, *The Negro Novel in America,* p. 84.

16. Clifford Mason, "Jean Toomer's Black Authenticity," *Black World* 20 (November 1970): 74.

17. Bone, *The Negro Novel in America,* p. 86.

18. In the Bible, wind and fire are manifestations of the Holy Spirit (e.g., *John* 3:8, and *Acts* 2:3 [Pentecost]).

19. Bone, *The Negro Novel in America,* p. 89.

20. Toomer, *Cane,* p. ix.

21. Arthur P. Davis, *From the Dark Tower: Afro-American Writers 1900 to 1960* (Washington, D.C.: Howard University Press, 1974), p. 51.

four

TWO POETIC GIANTS

The critics, especially the black press, tended to play off
Langston Hughes against Countee Cullen, praising the one and
damning the other. Some of the more astute judges, however,
recognized the striking differences between the work of these
two poets and appraised each on his own merits. These two
poetic giants of the Harlem Renaissance revealed their differences not only in their poetry but also in their literary criticism
of each other's works. The two young poets dominated the
realm of black poetry during the decade of the 1920s. We have,
in essence, the traditional romantic aesthete (Cullen) and the
genuine "New Negro" (Hughes), creating, even in their differences, a rhythmic, literary underpinning for the Negro craze
that rose and fell in the 1920s.

Langston Hughes was to emerge from the Harlem Renaissance as its chief literary artist and most famous survivor. Hughes

never moved out of Harlem; indeed, it was from Harlem that he drew his strength and nurtured his talent. As his most enduring character, Jesse B. Semple (known as Simple), said: "I love Harlem. . . . It's so full of Negroes. . . I feel like I got protection. . . . You say the houses ain't mine. Well the sidewalk is—and don't nobody push me off."[1] The tone and sentiment epitomize the attitude of the author and express, in a characteristic manner, the love and gratitude Hughes felt toward Harlem.

Langston Hughes relates his early life in *The Big Sea*, a narrative that is straightforward, yet not intimately frank, a life history that encompasses varied happenings to friends as well as to himself. Hughes was born in 1902 in Joplin, Missouri, but he was reared for the greater portion of his earliest years in Lawrence, Kansas. He came from a family typical of black Americans, especially at this time when a recognizable middle class was developing: he was descended from an interracial union (white and Indian, as well as Negro); his mother and her side of the family had modest means, whereas his father, separated from his mother and living in Mexico, was wealthy. It was the female side of the family that instilled in the young Hughes the virtues of honesty and forbearance—a heroic forbearance that Hughes exalted by showing his characters practicing their own brand of optimistic stoicism. From both sides of the family he learned pride, although his father's sickened him. Hughes recoiled from his father's hatred of his own race and the pride his father felt because he had escaped the fate of the American Negro and had succeeded economically as well. The Protestant work ethic practiced by the elder Hughes only added to the son's disenchantment with his father.

In 1921 Hughes entered Columbia University, resigned to getting an education because his father had been willing to finance it. The young poet was close to Harlem in any case. By the end of his first year in college the world away from Columbia was more intriguing and he quit his formal education for about four years. He traveled to Africa and Europe in search

of his roots and in search of adventure and freedom. When he
returned to the United States in 1924, he was a published
writer, known by readers of *The Crisis*. He was also broke.
But he eventually received aid from a patron. (Hughes recounts
in *The Big Sea* with some poignancy the entire relationship
between himself and·this unknown patron.)[2] With this help
he completed his college education at Lincoln University
where he was a student during "the height of the Negro Renaissance . . . spending my week-ends and holidays in New York."[3]
Hughes, indeed, was a child of the Harlem Renaissance.

In the 1925 *Opportunity* contest Hughes won the first prize
for poetry with "The Weary Blues," a poem he submitted as
an afterthought.[4] It has come to epitomize "jazz" or "blues"
poetry, and it was to represent the most authentic type of
black poetry until contemporary black poets started their
own literary revolution. "The Weary Blues" was like many of
the poems Hughes would come to be identified with: loose in
form, songful (indeed, the blues), idiomatic vocabulary, and
a tone that was without question negroid. Some critics were
outraged; one called "The Weary Blues" "a silly jingle."[5]
Hughes displayed in this prose-poem the qualities that would
dominate his verse throughout his career, as the following quo-
tations illustrate:

Jazz rhythms:

> Thump, thump, thump, went his foot on the floor.
> He played a few chords then he sang some more—
> "I got the Weary Blues
> And I can't be satisfied."[6]

Colloquial phrasing:

> Ain't got nobody in all this world,
> Ain't got nobody but ma self.
> I's gwine to quit ma frownin'
> And put ma troubles on the shelf. (23)

Vivid images:

> With his ebony hands on each ivory key
> He made that poor piano moan with melody.
> O Blues!
> Swaying to and fro on his rickety stool. (23)

In other poems written during this same period, there are humor and a touch of wild abandonment:

> Strut and wiggle,
> Shameless gal.
> Wouldn't no good fellow
> Be your pal. (20)

And there are poems of racial consciousness:

> I, too, sing America.
>
> I am the darker brother.
> They send me to eat in the kitchen
> When company comes.
> But I laugh,
> And eat well,
> And grow strong. (109)
>
> I've known rivers:
> I've known rivers ancient as the world and
> older than the flow of human blood in
> human veins.
> My soul has grown deep like the rivers. (51)

No other poet of the Harlem Renaissance captured in a similar mode the moods and emotions of the common black in the city, the Negro who was caught up in a repressive society alien to his soul. Hughes thrived on the life about him and translated

it into verse. In an article discussing the uses of poetry he wrote
that there should not be a "language gulf between poetry and
life."[7] Poetry, then, was not high art in Hughes's terms; rather,
it was a distillation, in rhythm, of the distinct black medley of
life. Interestingly, at a period when interest in "coloredness"
was registered at a seemingly infinite pitch, many found it difficult to accept Hughes's colloquial, jazzy poems. Not least among
his critics was his friend Countee Cullen who, in reviewing *The
Weary Blues*, wrote: "I regard the jazz poems as interlopers
in the company of the truly beautiful poems in other sections
of the book."[8]

The critical assaults, from both white and black reviewers,
had little effect upon Hughes. He continued to pursue that
avenue of expression he felt to be the true voice of blackness
and of Harlem in particular. In both of his early books, *The
Weary Blues* and *Fine Clothes to the Jew,* one is immediately
struck by his deep preoccupation with Negro existence, mores,
and manners; his poetry is an extension of the life he lived and
witnessed. Once, in an interview, Hughes stated that the major
aim of his writing was "to interpret and comment upon Negro
life, and its relation to the problems of Democracy."[9] What
we have, then, is a poet who has so immersed himself in the
experiences of his people that his commentaries about life are
shared revelations instead of self-analysis.

A characteristic of many of Hughes's poems is the affirmation of life, either stated or implied, displayed thematically or
dramatically. Hughes insisted on this affirmation despite his
knowledge (which he strongly depicted in his verse) of the difficulties the black man faced in this inequitable world:

> White ones, brown ones,
> What do you know
> About tomorrow
> Where all paths go?

Jazz-boys, jazz-boys,—
Play, play, PLAY!
Tomorrow . . . is darkness,
Joy today. (32)

And again:

Weary,
Weary,
Trouble, pain.
Sun's gonna shine
Somewhere
Again. (37)

In *The Weary Blues,* Hughes explicates and extols the cabaret life in Harlem. The title poem is one example; another is a verse entitled "Cabaret." Some of these poems are full of raucousness and total abandon:

EVERYBODY
Half-pint,—
Gin?
No, make it
LOVES MY BABY
Corn. You like
liquor,
don't you, honey? (27)

But then his tender side emerges and he writes of a young singer in a poem of the same title and, after stating that she sings "Chansons vulgaires," terminates with the quiet image "That she is like a nymph/ For some wild faun" (28).

There are two distinct features that are central to an understanding of Hughes's early work: the use of jazz and the blues, and interjection of the "shout," which is derived from black religion.

In a brief note at the beginning of *Fine Clothes to the Jew*,
Hughes wrote the following explication of his "blues" poems:
"The *Blues*, unlike the *Spirituals*, have a strict poetic pattern:
one long line repeated and a third line to rhyme with the first
two. Sometimes the second line in repetition is slightly changed
and sometimes, but very seldom, it is omitted. The mood of
the *Blues* is almost always despondency, but when they are
sung people laugh."[10] This style was suited perfectly to the
genre of poetry that was attempting to speak for the common
black man living in a workaday world. The life he was describing was away from literary salons, a world away from Park
Avenue patrons who found Negro life quaint and exotic. The
world of Hughes's poems was closer to the one in which he
lived and wrote in those early, lean years. As he relates in his
autobiography, most of the poems "were written while I was
dragging bags of wet wash laundry about or toting trays of
dirty dishes to the dumb-waiter of the Wardman Park Hotel
in Washington."[11]

This first distinct feature of Hughes's poetry, then, the metaphor of music—jazz and the blues—is a vital mode for expressing the unique quality of Negro life. In almost romantic terms,
Hughes once declared, "Jazz to me is one of the inherent expressions of Negro life in America."[12] And in his poem, "Lenox
Avenue: Midnight," he writes:

> The rhythm of life
> Is a jazz rhythm. (39)

Hughes seems to intimate that the spiritual struggle of the
black man to emancipate himself from the restraints and mech-
anization of civilization can be expressed best through the
idiom of music—music that is played or music that is imitated
through the beat and language of poetry.

The other distinct characteristic of Hughes's poetry, the
"shout," is mentioned by the poet in his autiobiography. This

device, J. Saunders Redding states, "takes its name from the single line of strophic and incremental significance which is shouted or moaned after each two, three, or four line stanza."[13] Hughes employs this technique in such poems as "Judgment Day" and "Moan." The use of the repetitive "Fire" in the poem of the same name is a variant of the "shout."

In these ways, Hughes was able to exhibit his concern for experimentation, in form more so than in language. The use of jazz rhythms, the tone and lilt of spirituals, and the adaptation of the "shout" inform his poetry with the overall effect of having captured the spirit of common Negro life. His poetry is written in a spare, direct language that grasps an emotion and a mood immediately; there is no standing back in order to weave the language into complex patterns. A strong rhythmic sense and the natural Negro idiom serve each other in a fashion to create a folksy, guileless poetry. Hughes may not have been the intellectual's poet, but he was highly creative.

The basic emotion sustaining Hughes's drive to write about the common black folk was love. His undeviating love for his people and his town, Harlem, was *sui generis* even during this period of Negromania. Hughes never lost this love, nor did he modify it as he might have when his success and popularity made it possible for him to live in any section of New York. It is safe to say, also, that long before the notion of *Négritude* was formulated into definitions by Césaire and Senghor, Hughes had defined it through his poetry: his evocation of both a timeless unity between all blacks and the *élan vital* of African life and culture gives proof of this observation. "I've known rivers:/ Ancient, dusky rivers./ My soul has grown deep like the rivers" (51). What better way to express the eternal black soul? Or, "I am a Negro:/Black as the night is black/ Black like the depths of my Africa" (19). Later, in his famous, much-quoted poem, "Harlem," we hear the lines, "What happens to the dream deferred?/ Does it dry up/ like a raisin in the sun?"[14] In these lines are the frustration and disappointment sensed by blacks in Harlem and the microcosmic world of the black in

America. In his constant blend of the tones of black melancholy or black laughter and the idiom of the natural street jargon, Hughes produces an authentic brand of black American poetry.

Hughes possessed an unrestrained immediacy that permitted him to enrich his contemporary-styled poems with the felt heritage of group soul. His mind spanned the ages in a chorus of black sounds. By leaping back into the past, in order to connect it with the present, Hughes displayed a range of emotions that were often juxtaposed: pain and pleasure, joy and sorrow, despair and hope. His poetry, then, exhibits a sure control of tone; the various inflections create unmistakable moods that are understood immediately on an emotional level. It was precisely his tendency to value emotion over the intellect, or at least a fusion of the two into a less personal sort of poem, that caused one critic to say of Hughes: "He feels in them [his poems], but he does not think."[15] Hughes, however, pursued the writing of black poetry with scant worry about what his critics, either white or black, wrote. In a later justification of his attitude, he wrote: "I didn't pay any attention to the critics who railed against the subject matter of my peoms, nor did I write them protesting letters, nor in any way attempt to defend my book. Curiously enough, a short ten years later, many of those very poems in *Fine Clothes to the Jew* were being used in Negro schools and colleges."[16]

Countee Cullen was quite another matter. When his first book of poetry, *Color*, appeared in 1925, he received lavish accolades. One English reviewer went so far as to say: "If there is a more promising poet in America, I do not know his name. . . . Countee Cullen is a supreme master of Beauty."[17] In general, the critics tended to deemphasize the racial themes of his poetry despite the title of the book and despite Cullen's subtle preoccupation with the subject. Cullen was, after all, a child of the Harlem Renaissance, and he felt as deep a need for enriching the present through the racial past as did his more

spontaneous friend, Langston Hughes. Where Hughes stressed
the common black man's vigor and contempt for restraint,
Cullen emphasized the black man's grandeur:

> And now it was of bitterness and death,
> The cry the lash exhorts, the broken breath
> Of liberty enchained; and yet there ran
> Through all a harmony of faith in man,
> A knowledge all would end as it began.
> All sights and sounds and aspects of my race
> Accompanied this melody, kept pace
> With it; with music all their hopes and hates
> Were charged, not to be downed by all the fates.
> And somehow it was borne upon my brain
> How being dark, and living through the pain
> Of it, is courage more than angels have.[18]

So the interest in race was there. He never abandoned this
theme, although it is also important to realize that this was
just one of his poetic preoccupations. Because of Cullen's
character, upbringing, and inclinations toward the nineteenth-
century English Romantics, he could not escape the themes of
love, and the deep drive toward the evocation of beauty.
Cullen's favorite poet was John Keats, and this interest more
than any other influence both inspired and hampered the
artist in Countee Cullen.

Cullen was born in New York City in 1903 and was educated
in the public schools in Harlem and then in the Bronx at DeWitt-
Clinton High School. It was during this time that his first poem,
"To the Swimmer," was published.[19] He followed this first
effort with an extensive outpouring of poetry and three stories
that were published in his high school literary journal, *The
Magpie.* By the time Cullen graduated from New York University he was a fairly well-known poet. He went directly to

Harvard to work on his master's degree in French, and while he was there his first book, *Color*, was published. The road to fame was without question an easy one for Cullen, for nearly everything he had submitted to editors had been published when this initial collection appeared.

The ease with which he was accepted as a poet may have been a deterrent to maturation in his handling of theme, tone, and style. His work is marred by archaic expressions and evocation of an everlasting *weltschmerz*. The lyrical strain in his poetry is strong, and it is not surprising to find that he admired poets such as Millay, Housman, and E. A. Robinson. He was, indeed, as Jay Saunders Redding described him, a poet who "cannot beat the tom-tom above a faint whisper."[20] Yet he wanted to discover and to evoke the rich past of the black man. He did this in a subdued and restrained manner, however. The lyric line is never absent:

> Her walk is like the replica
> Of some barbaric dance
> Wherein the soul of Africa
> Is winged with arrogance. (4)

Or,

> The cries of all dark people near or far
> Were billowed over me, a mighty surge
> Of suffering in which my puny grief must merge
> And lose itself; I had no further claim to urge
> For death. (22)

Cullen was also obsessed with love and death—the joy of love and the sorrow of love and the inevitability of death. Still, Cullen, perhaps because of his upbringing in a religious atmosphere, viewed death as not only an end but a beginning (e.g., "They lie who say that death is worse"[21]; and "Dead men are wisest, for they know/ How far the roots of flowers go"[40]).

The ambivalency in Cullen's theological beliefs is apparent
in all of his work. One senses this strongly in both of his best-
known poems, "Heritage" and "Yet Do I Marvel." In the latter
poem, the opening lines express inevitable submission to the
traditional significance of God, i.e., that He is basically the
symbol of and indeed the true, unsullied epitome of goodness.
Yet, in His inscrutable ways, He permits unfathomable cruel-
ties to be inflicted on mortals. The poet, however, can ultimately
understand these things because, as he says, if God would "stoop
to quibble" (3), an explanation would be forthcoming. What is
more difficult to comprehend, then, is God's nerve in creating
a black man who must also be a poet: "Yet do I marvel at this
curious thing:/ To make a poet black, and bid him sing!" Cullen
sees a conceit in this anomaly, inasmuch as the black man is a
scorned being, a being looked upon by some as subhuman. Yet,
this same man is compelled to write poetry, an art form deriving
from a superior mind.

Thus God both performs a miracle and creates an ironic
situation. In so doing, He places an added burden on the black
poet, the onus of uniqueness in addition to his assigned role
as a pariah in society. Is Cullen mocking God? Or is the poet
directing anger towards God? Is there, in other words, more
irony than despair in the poem? Cullen has given us a paradox
within a paradox.

Cullen was also obsessed with love and death—the joy of love
poet, not as a Negro poet. He consciously strove to imbue his
poetry with the form, syntax, and mode of expression found
in the poetry Americans inherited or adapted from their Anglo-
Saxon heritage. Certainly Cullen was successful in many of his
poems of this nature, and he, at least, did not find it inappro-
priate to adapt this genre of poetry to verses that were racial
in theme. *The Black Christ* (not one of his more successful
productions) is ample proof. And despite his avowal to write
poetry simply as a man rather than as a black man, he did
admit that "in spite of myself. . . . I find that I am actuated
by a strong sense of race consciousness."[22]

When his last book of poetry, *On These I Stand,* was published posthumously in 1947, critics attempted to assess Cullen's poetry of the past twenty years. There was disappointment that he had not fulfilled his early promise, that he had "neither accepted nor developed a comprehensive worldview."[23] Cullen rather exemplifies the Negro described in DuBois's *The Souls of Black Folk:* "One ever feels his twoness,—an American, a Negro; two souls, two thoughts, two unreconciled strivings; two warring ideals in one dark body. . . . The history of the American Negro is the history of this strife,—this longing to attain self-conscious manhood, to merge his double self into a better and truer self."[24] In his desire to be assessed as a poet with his own unique cultural heritage (the black, the African), Cullen hovered on the brink of racial writing. That is, he chose subjects and metaphors of blackness but he never seemed to submerge his personal self into the act of most of these creations. Perhaps he was inhibited by the haunting cry in his own famous lines:

> Yet do I marvel at this curious thing:
> To make a poet black, and bid him sing!

Hughes and Cullen were in harmony in their desire to promulgate not only their own artistic work but that of other black writers as well. The one-issue publication, *Fire,* appeared in 1926 largely through their efforts and those of others, such as Wallace Thurman. *Fire* contained Cullen's rather conventional "From the Dark Tower," as well as a story by Bruce Nugent that Hughes described as "a green and purple story." The black critics condemned the whole publication as too daring, and most white critics, except the one in *The Bookman*, ignored the magazine's existence. In the end, most of the copies, which were being held in warehouse storage, were destroyed in an accidental fire. The importance of the magazine lies in the fact that young black artists attempted to present their diverse works in their own mode and under their own auspices. From an artistic viewpoint, therefore, the venture was a success.

In 1926, Hughes's famous essay, "The Negro Artist and the Racial Mountain," appeared in *The Nation*. It was a swaggering artistic manifesto in which he took Cullen to task: "One of the most promising of the young Negro poets said to me once, 'I want to be a poet—not a Negro poet,' meaning, I believe, 'I would like to write like a white poet'; meaning behind that, 'I would like to be white.' "[25] Hughes, honest and characteristically unsplenetic in his criticism, attacked two predominant attitudes among many Negroes: (1) that one must propagandize through presenting "better qualities" in Negro life, in order to prove that some Negroes differed from whites only because of skin color; and, closely related to this sentiment, (2) that one should write in a style that was indistinguishable from that of the white artist, except for the subject matter. (One could, however, as Paul Laurence Dunbar had done, write about whites as well as blacks.) To Hughes, these ideas were spiritual and artistic anathema: "no great poet has ever been afraid of being himself. . . . But this is the mountain standing in the way of any true Negro art in America—this urge within the race toward whiteness, the desire to pour racial individuality into the mold of American standardization, and to be as little Negro and as much American as possible."[26]

Hughes was not merely making an apology for his own defined preoccupations—the blues, jazz, the black man's "ironic laughter mixed with tears"; he was also trying to explain why it was necessary for the black artist to be unashamed to express his blackness. If the black artist pursued his own path, perhaps he would eventually make the world understand and appreciate his work. If people—black or white, fellow-artist or not—were not pleased, it didn't matter, for, as Hughes expressed it, "We build our temples for tomorrow, strong as we know how, and we stand on top of the mountain, free within ourselves."[27]

Hughes and Cullen took divergent approaches as they continued to produce poetry that received considerable attention from the critics. But their contrasting responses, artistically, to the role of the black poet in America served to call more attention to the Harlem Renaissance movement itself. And certainly by the time Hughes's essay reverberated through the literary community and *Fire* kindled and fizzled, there seemed to be little question that a full-blown movement was in progress. The major poets gave it fame, but the novels that appeared sustained the movement. Both Hughes and Cullen rallied to this notion and managed to produce good fiction in addition to their poetry. The dimensions of the Harlem Renaissance were not to be contained, and the two giants of black American literature moved forward with the age.

NOTES

1. Langston Hughes, *The Best of Simple* (New York: Hill & Wang, 1961), p. 20.

2. According to Zora Neale Hurston, she and Hughes shared the same patron—Mrs. R. Osgood Mason. See Zora Neale Hurston, *Dust Tracks on a Road* (Philadelphia: Lippincott, 1942), p. 185.

3. Langston Hughes, *The Big Sea* (New York: Hill & Wang, c. 1940), p. 278.

4. Ibid., p. 215.

5. *Boston Chronicle*, 30 May 1925.

6. Langston Hughes, *The Weary Blues* (New York: Knopf, 1944), p. 23. All subsequent quotes will be from this edition and will have page numbers indicated in the text.

7. Langston Hughes, "Ten Ways to Use Poetry in Teaching," *CLA Journal* 10 (1968): 275.

8. *Opportunity* 4 (February 1926): 73.

9. *Phylon* 7 (4th Quarter, 1950): 307.

10. Langston Hughes, *Fine Clothes to the Jew* (New York: Knopf, 1927), p. xiii.

11. Hughes, *The Big Sea*, pp. 271-272.

12. Langston Hughes, "The Negro Artist and the Racial Mountain," *The Nation* 122 (23 June 1926): 693.

13. J. Saunders Redding, *To Make a Poet Black* (Chapel Hill: University of North Carolina Press, 1939), pp. 115-116.

14. Arnold Adoff, *The Poetry of Black America: Anthology of the Twentieth Century* (New York: Harper & Row, 1973), p. 76.

15. Redding, *To Make a Poet Black*, p. 116.

16. Hughes, *The Big Sea*, p. 268.

17. *International Book Review* 4 (March 1926): 252.

18. Countee Cullen, *On These I Stand* (New York: Harper, 1947), pp. 21-22. All subsequent quotes will be from this edition and will have page numbers indicated in the text.

19. "To the Swimmer" was published in *Modern School* (May 1918) under the name with which he was born. He was adopted in 1918 by the Reverend Frederick A. Cullen.

20. Redding, *To Make a Poet Black*, p. 111.

21. Langston Hughes and Arna Bontemps, eds., *Poetry of the Negro, 1746-1949* (Garden City: Doubleday, 1949), p. 131.

22. *New York Times*, 2 December 1923, sec. 2, p. 1.

23. *Poetry* 70 (July 1947): 223.

24. W. E. Burghardt DuBois, *The Souls of Black Folk* (Greenwich, Conn.: Fawcett, c. 1961), p. 17.

25. Langston Hughes, "The Negro Artist and the Racial Mountain," p. 693.

26. Ibid.

27. Ibid.

five

THE MAJOR NOVELS

There were no novels by Harlem Renaissance writers of major importance in general American literature during the 1920s. All of the black writers were in the massive shadow of literary luminaries such as Hemingway, Fitzgerald, and Sinclair Lewis. There were novels of major and minor importance, however, among black writers; every principal writer produced at least one novel during the years 1924-1932. The release of artistic expression gathered momentum beginning in 1924 when *The Crisis* and *Opportunity* announced creative writing contests and Jessie Fauset and Walter White published their first novels. In 1927, for instance, the black literary output was an unchecked flow of poetry and prose that wound in and around periodicals and publishing houses on the eastern literary scene. Rudolph Fisher had six short stories which appeared throughout the year, Cullen edited a collection of poetry by

Negroes, *Caroling Dusk*, and two of his own books of poetry, *Copper Sun* and *The Ballad of the Brown Girl*, appeared. Hughes's second book, *Fine Clothes to the Jew*, gave the black press an outlet for denouncing a movement that could not now be stopped. On the other hand, the publication of James Weldon Johnson's *God's Trombones* drew praise from the critics even though he anticipated a chorus of rebuke from them because he consciously avoided dialect. One may safely assert that in the year 1927 dialect was declared dead. (One important exception, of course, was the work of Sterling Brown.)

The prevailing notion of the fiction of the Harlem Renaissance writers during the 1920s was that it exaggerated the more offensive qualities of low-life in the black ghetto—drink, sex, gambling, violence, and exotic behavior. The truth is that the literature spanning the period of the Harlem Renaissance, roughly from 1923 through 1932, focused on *every* aspect of black life. The portrayal of low-life was part of the trend toward freeing readers from seeing the black person as a problem; it was also an attempt to portray blackness with a candor that the newer writers felt had been lacking in the literature of the past. In fiction, several angles of black life were explored in order to emphasize the harsh injustice of prejudice, the basic human worth of the black race, the bourgeois life of blacks, the irrepressible spontaneity and vitality of the race, and the search for a common heritage, so that, in the words of Countee Cullen, blacks would not have to sing:

> What is last year's snow to me,
> Last year's anything? The tree
> Budding yearly must forget
> How its past arose or set—
>
> . . . .
>
> *One three centuries removed*
> *From the scenes his fathers loved,*
> *Spicy grove, cinnamon tree,*
> *What is Africa to me?*[1].

The overall controlling symbol of blackness formed the basis for the major themes explored in the fiction and poetry of the Harlem Renaissance writers. In various plot modes and poetic outpourings, the themes of passing, miscegenation, the "tragic mulatto," the Negro's struggle for self-assertion, violence (mostly white), forms of prejudice (white against black, black against black), and the vitality of the Negro were recurrent in the works of these young writers. Some of the works were in the form of propaganda; some offerings bordered on or succumbed to the cult of exoticism; still other works presented a realistic portrayal of Negro life. The novel, of course, was the perfect vehicle for exploring all of the concerns which the Negro writer wished to portray and explicate.

The mediocre novels written by Negroes (e.g., Herman Dreer, Mary Etta Spencer) who preceded the Harlem Renaissance novelists were not immediately replaced by examples of high art. After all, the oral tradition was still the most potent influence on the black artist. The unique need felt by some to propagandize through fiction also hindered other writers from recognizing and employing the better tools of fiction. The body of Harlem Renaissance novels, therefore, is unevenly chiseled, but the primary aim of all Negro novelists, regardless of their style or thematic preoccupation, was to act as truthful interpreters of the black race for the reading public. No longer would there be the fiction of distortion, created by writers who lacked knowledge of the black world or who actually believed in the existing black stereotypes. The Negro novelist of the past, Chesnutt and Dunbar included, had sometimes succumbed to the same easy habits of the white writers in portraying the Negro in caricature. A conscious attempt was made during the 1920s and early 1930s to rid readers of the idea that the black character was a little less than human or so pious and patient in the face of oppression that he achieved an otherworldly sanctification that strained credibility. The one character that the Harlem Renaissance writers seemed unable (or, perhaps, unwilling) to purge from their postbellum literary heritage was the "tragic mulatto." Of course, it can be argued, without straining too greatly, that this type was a real part of the everyday world the Negro writer of the 1920s knew.

To grasp the intent of the various writers and to understand how they attempted to articulate their concerns through artistic expression, individual novels must be examined. The working out of themes and the crystallization of black life and culture were abundant in the novels of the following writers: Rudolph Fisher, Claude McKay, Nella Larsen, James Weldon Johnson, Countee Cullen, and Langston Hughes, whose works will be discussed in this chapter. The novels of Wallace Thurman, Jessie Fauset, Walter White, W. E. B. DuBois, Arna Bontemps, and George Schuyler will be discussed in the next chapter.

Rudolph Fisher was a literary craftsman who understood and practiced such arts of fiction as control over plot, characterization, tone, and language, and who had a natural poise in exposition. Fisher was as at ease writing novels as he was writing short stories, although the short stories are of greater artistic quality. Fisher is one of those writers about whom one would like to speculate, "If only he had lived longer"; even so, his accomplishments by 1934 (he died in December of that year) were far from negligible. His first novel, *The Walls of Jericho*, for instance, contains one of the most amusing yet cynical scenes (the Merritt-Cramp conversation) in modern literature. He was the first black writer to have a creditable and absorbing mystery published in America (*The Conjure-man Dies*). As a stylist, Fisher had no peer among the nonexperimental Harlem Renaissance writers. This skill, however, led to his most notable weakness—a clever adroitness that makes his satire somewhat strained in some instances, and, related to this, a feather-light style that sometimes blurs his dramatic impact.

The Walls of Jericho (1928) is a study in black realistic fiction, for Fisher follows closely the dictum of Henry James in giving his novel an "air of reality" (as opposed to representing life) through his concern with mimesis rather than theme and form. (This is stated merely for contrast, not in terms of exclusion; Fisher was certainly concerned, as a stylist, with form, and as a man caught up in the spirit of the Harlem Renaissance, he was not oblivious to the importance of theme and motif.) An early commentator on the Harlem Renaissance wrote about Fisher:

> [His] realism does not go searching after exotic places, but walks the streets of Harlem with its lowly. His interest dwells upon transplanted southern country folk who, having reached the city, have not yet had bound upon their natures the *aes triplex* of city sophistication. They are simple, funloving folk, sometimes religious, more usually superstitious, leaning ardently toward the good but not too zealously to be sometimes led astray by bewildering temptations.[2]

There is a plot and subplot in *The Walls of Jericho*, where all strata of Negro society in New York City are represented— the uneducated lower classes (but not the poverty-stricken), the gamblers, the middle class, and the so-called upper class. The hero, Ralph Merrit, a lawyer by profession, can be counted among the few in this last category.[3] He is, in the words of the common Negro, a "dickty," and he receives little support or sympathy at the opening of the book where it is revealed that he has bought a house in a white neighborhood just bordering on Harlem. Despite this move, the extremely pale (but kinky-haired) Merrit has none of the pretentions often present in Negroes of his class, even though it is assumed that he does by the characters Fisher presents in contrast to him—Shine (Joshua Jones), and Jinx and Bubber (Fisher's black Damon and Pythias). As a matter of fact, Merrit's reason for moving into the white neighborhood is not obvious. As he explains:

> All of you know where I stand on things racial—I'm down-right rabid. And even though . . . I'd enjoy this house, if they let me alone, purely as an individual, just the same I'm entering it as a Negro. I hate fays. Always have. Always will. Chief joy in life is making them uncomfortable. And if this doesn't do it—I'll quit the bar.[4]

Side by side with the story of Merrit is the romance between Shine and the Negro maid, Linda. She works for Miss Cramp, a bigoted neighbor of Merrit, who sees herself as an enlightened benefactor of the downtrodden and misguided. Miss Cramp takes on causes the way sticky tape picks up lint, and her interest is as short-lived as lint-covered adhesive is useful. Her arrogant notions of racial superiority are mitigated only by her evident obtuseness and sheer ignorance. Such a restricted, narrow mind is beyond repair, as her name implies: she stands as a symbol of the blind, bigoted do-gooder who clutters the world with unproductive activities and confused motives. She is also unfortunately a victim of Fisher's penchant for carica-ture; the light touch he applies to Miss Cramp lessens the magni-tude of what she really symbolizes. Still, it is possible that her name will become as meaningful to the literate reader as the name Babbitt, thereby enriching the descriptive language of America.

The work companions, Shine, Jinx, and Bubber, provide the book with comic characters and also furnish the reader with an insight into staple personalities in black society—persons who are (or, perhaps, were) rarely seen outside of Harlem (at least, in their true character) and therefore remain a mystery to the white world. To citizens of Harlem, the prototypes of Jinx and Bubber were in evidence daily. They add as much to an air of reality as do the places described in the various scenes. Both men conform analogically to the black joker hero and, in a more tenuous fashion, to the trickster hero.

Thematically, Fisher was concerned with the idea of black unity and the discovery of self. He uses the Bible story of Joshua to reinforce his concern for the black man's search for his true nature that will permit him to disengage himself from the deceptions of the past. Every man is Joshua, facing a seem-ingly impenetrable wall:

No man knows himself till he comes to an impasse; to some strange set of conditions that reveals to him his ignorance of the workings of his spirit; to some disrupting impact that

shatters the wall of self-illusion. This, I believe, is the greatest
spiritual battle of a man's life, the battle with his own idea
of himself. (185-186)

It is such knowledge that draws divergent segments of the black
population—the Ralph Merrits and the Joshua Joneses—into a
unity that can do battle with the white enemy inside the walls
of Jericho.

Fisher's second book, *The Conjure-man Dies* (1932), is the
first black detective novel published in the United States. The
book was an important addition to the literature of the Harlem
Renaissance because it exhibited again Fisher's abiding interest
in his race and the formulation of ties with the African homeland. Fisher believed that Harlem was a natural setting for the
mystery novel:

> Darkness and mystery go together, don't they? The children
> of the night—and I say this in all seriousness—are children of
> mystery. The very setting is mystery—outsiders know nothing
> of Harlem life as it really is . . . what goes on behind the
> scenes and beneath the dark skins of Harlem folk—fiction
> has not found much of that yet. And much of it is perfectly
> in tune with the best of mystery tradition—variety, color,
> mysticism, superstition, malice and violence.[5]

The semicomic Jinx and Bubber appear in this book also.
They liven the action and the conversation, contributing some
touches of comic relief to the peculiar, mysterious atmosphere.
They were Fisher's favorite characters, "who," as he said,
"having shared several adventures with me before, have become
very real to me."[6]

Fisher was also fascinated by the technique of contructing
a mystery novel—the mingling of fact and fiction, and the opportunity to commence what was to have become, had Fisher lived,
a corpus of detective novels known as the Dart-Archer series.
In discussing *The Conjure-man Dies*, Fisher stated: "An archer,

of course, is a bowman, one who shoots an arrow. Dart is another word for arrow. Dr. Archer and Detective Dart, therefore, stand in the relationship of a bowman and his arrow; the
vision of the former gives direction and aim to the action of
the latter."[7] The book also gave Fisher a grand chance not only
to vivify Harlem as a place of clubs and cabarets but to portray
it as the home of the ordinary black folk who supply most of
its color and movement.

When Claude McKay died in 1948, it was noted that "it was
a request of Mr. McKay that his funeral service be held in Harlem, where he spent so much of his active life."[8] McKay spent
the years between 1922 and 1934 out of the United States, but
the memory of Harlem and all that it meant to him, both symbolically and sensually, never faded from his mind, even when
he had lost some of his younger fervor for its haunts.

McKay was damned as a novelist by DuBois and others (even
James Weldon Johnson did not like *Home to Harlem*) who felt
that McKay exploited the theme of Negro primitivism and
leaned too heavily on the effects of exotic descriptions of low-
life. The formless aspect of his narratives was also disconcert-
ing. This was so even though he included, for example, a sub-
title, "A story without a plot," on the title page of the novel
Banjo. The formlessness, therefore, was clearly intentional.

One of McKay's assets was his unambivalent attitude toward
race: he was a black man and he was proud of it. He wasn't
interested in assimilation, although he had a forceful streak of
the European aesthete in him which he neither exalted nor
damned. He once wrote: "Whatever may be the criticism implied
in my writing of Western civilization I do not regard myself as
a stranger but as a child of it, even though I may have become
so by the comparatively recent process of grafting. I am as conscious of my new-world birthright as of my African origin, being
aware of the one and its significance in my development as
much as I feel the other emotionally."[9] This dualistic sentiment
did not mean that he was not conscious of the problem his

color presented. One must not forget McKay's own admission that "my main psychological problem . . . was the problem of color. Color-consciousness was the fundamental of my restlessness."[10] McKay was satisfied with his own understanding of himself and his dual heritage; what saddened and often exasperated him was the lack of understanding he found among whites who could not envision how a man as civilized as McKay could refuse to accept the European, Anglo-Saxon value system. This dualism, a problem not to be solved by a simple statement incorporating the idea that the black race had a respectable past, one different from whites but equal to it in terms of the values that were transmitted from one generation to the next, was simply one more result of the white man's refusal to legitimize black experience. As McKay saw it, then, the problem really wasn't his alone; the white person had to share the responsibility for placing McKay, and others like him, in two worlds. And when one exists in two worlds, one can hardly be completely loyal to either of them. McKay understood this, but many of his critics, he surmised, did not.

A spiritual and intellectual cleavage existed as well between McKay and the black bourgeois writers of the Harlem Renaissance. McKay was keenly aware of the inner struggles of the younger black writers.[11] Thus, he portrays his concern about every aspect of blackness, the black soul, and the "new Negro" through Ray, who becomes his spokesman in both of his vagabond novels. These same concerns are also a part of his autobiography, *A Long Way from Home* (1937).

When *Home to Harlem* appeared in 1928, McKay was accused of being too greatly influenced by Van Vechten's *Nigger Heaven*. McKay defended himself against this unsubstantiated charge when his book first appeared; later, in his autobiography, he explained:

Many persons imagine that I wrote *Home to Harlem* because Carl Van Vechten wrote *Nigger Heaven*. But the pattern of the book was written under the title of "Home to Harlem"

in 1925. When Max Eastman read it he said, "It is worth a
thousand dollars." Under the same title it was entered in
the story contest of the Negro magazine *Opportunity*. But
it did not excite the judges. *Nigger Heaven* was published
in the fall of 1926. I never saw the book until the late spring
of 1927, when my agent . . . sent me a copy. And by that
time I had nearly completed *Home to Harlem*. [12]

This explanation ought to be accepted not only because it
seems convincing but also because both novels are each so different that the question of Van Vechten's influence becomes
academic.

Home to Harlem is a vagabond novel, full of color, noise,
and vitality, rounded out by a touch of intellectualism and
social criticism. The story is loosely structured around the
search by Jake, the primary character, for the "tantalizing
brown" whom he enjoys on his first night in that home of
homes for the black man, Harlem. Jake is home from the war—
the white man's war—an *AWOL* with a taste for English-made
suits, an uncomplicated sensualist who lives each day to its
fullest. He is the archetypal primitive who will never succumb
to the restraints of Puritan American civilization. At the end
of the novel, he finds his girl (who, by the way, left him the
$50.00 during that first joyful night) and discovers her name
which, quite appropriately, is Felice ("Joy"). While the movement from beginning to end is episodic and disjointed, the
novel is successful in: (1) its portrayal of life in Harlem's
cabarets, rent parties, pool rooms, and other dives of the more
lowly; (2) its exposure of the mentality and weaknesses of
bourgeois life; (3) its exploration of the problems of the Negro
intellectual (i.e., a person overly cultivated in norms alien to
his origins and, therefore, an unhappy disaffected individual);
and (4) its examination of the nature and place of sex in the
black world.

It is an antithetical world which McKay paints, a world
rendered in disjointed sentences, slang, and elliptical Negro

phrases that ring with authenticity. There may be a little exaggeration, but McKay's contrast of a world within a world requires some overstatement. The antithesis is also internal, for his aim in presenting characters like Ray and Jake is not to juxtapose opposing elements of society but, more important, to give two sides of the contradictory nature of man: sensual man vs. sensible man.

This kind of probing is an important element in McKay's novel *Banjo* (1929). Ray is also a key character in this book, and Jake is replaced by his counterpart, the Banjo of the title. The book is peopled with men and women who inhabit the fringes of "respectable" society. They live around the waterfront in Marseilles where their existence is a combination of the grim, the grimy, and the happy-go-lucky. The most important segments of the book deal with Ray's tirades against the black American for his aping of whites and discursive conversations that explain McKay's sentiments about the Harlem Renaissance. Here, for instance, is Ray talking to a Martiniquan student:

'In the modern race of life we're merely beginners. If this renaissance we're talking about is going to be more than a sporadic and scabby thing, we'll have to get down to our racial roots to create it.'
'I believe in a racial renaissance," said the student, 'but not in going back to savagery.'
'Getting down to our native roots and building up from our own people,' said Ray, 'is not savagery. It is culture.'
'I can't see that,' said the student.
'You are like many Negro intellectuals who are bellyaching about race,' said Ray. 'What's wrong with you all is your education. You get a white man's education and learn to despise your own people. . . .
'You're a lost crowd, you educated Negroes, and you will find yourself in the roots of your own people.'[13]

From such episodes, something can be learned about McKay as Ray's attitudes waver from bitterness to tenderness to moral confusion. At the book's end Ray retains some of his ambivalence, although he makes a positive choice to remain, at least for a time, in the sensual world. His decision, then, is made with an air of one who is still experimenting with notions of how to live one's life.

McKay's last novel, *Banana Bottom* (1933), is not within the basic time or thematic scope of this book and will not be discussed. In one critic's view it "is the first classic of West Indian prose."[14] The West Indian tone and mood prevail in McKay's collection of short stories, too, although the Harlem stories have greater artistic strength. *Gingertown* (1932) contains twelve examples of McKay's short fiction. The Harlem tales, in particular, give an intimate and vivid portrait of Renaissance Harlem. For example, "Brownskin Blues," a story of another Mary Lou (Thurman's), is about a woman whose black skin leads to tragedy. "Mattie and Her Sweetman" portrays the life of an older woman who is supporting a young man. In both of these stories, crude as they are, McKay exhibits control over his characterizations and the setting. "High Ball" is another of his successful tales, in terms of theme and characterization; the protagonist, Nation, is sympathetically and realistically portrayed (see Chapter 7 for further discussion of this story). In this story McKay explores a virulent form of race prejudice and expresses one aspect of the black man's struggle for self-assertion. Curiously, the West Indian tales are the weakest in the book, but they are written with such a lyrical nostalgia that the stories have a unique, seductive quality.

McKay's importance in the Harlem Renaissance is undisputed, even though he was physically absent from the United States during its height. His almost obsessive concern with the nature of contradiction in the black man's character compelled him to write fiction and poetry which embrace many of the earmarks of Harlem Renaissance literature.

McKay, like Cullen, was unable to fulfill his potential, although the body of McKay's work is not unimpressive. What seems to be lacking in his work is a certain breadth which he might have displayed if he had continued in the direction in which he started when he wrote *Banana Bottom*. In it he seems to have turned to another level of expression, the orthodox novel, but he ceased producing significant artistic literature at this point in his life. Stephen H. Bronz assesses McKay in this perceptive summation of his role in the Harlem Renaissance:

> Because McKay was not fully a member of any one group, and because of his radical education and outspoken personality, he set the outer limits of the Harlem Renaissance. No other important Negro writer in the 'twenties protested so fiercely and single-mindedly against prejudice as did McKay in his sonnets of 1919. And no other important Renaissance figure disregarded possible effects on the Negro public image so fearlessly as did McKay in his prose fiction. From his Jamaican days to his strange conversion to Catholicism, McKay forever spoke his mind, sometimes brilliantly, sometimes clumsily, but always forthrightly. In so doing he did much to make the Harlem Renaissance more than a polite attempt to show whites that Negroes, too, could be cultured.[15]

Robert Bone places Nella Larsen, along with Jessie Fauset, W. E. B. DuBois, and Walter White, in the class of "The Rear Guard," that is, "novelists [who] still wished to orient Negro art toward white opinion. They wished to apprise educated whites of the existence of respectable Negroes, and to call their attention—now politely, now indignantly—to facts of racial injustice."[16]

Nella Larsen was a descendant of two widely different racial and cultural backgrounds: her father was a West Indian Negro and her mother was Danish. Larsen's own origins and the subsequent unfulfilled life she led as the wife of an adulterer (whom

she finally divorced) provided her with the material for her life's
work. Certainly she followed the admonition to young writers
to "write what you know about" in her first novel, *Quicksand*.
The theme of the tragic mulatto is merged with what Bone
describes as the basic metaphor of the novel which is "contained in its title [and] supported throughout by concrete
images of suffocation, asphyxiation, and claustrophobia."[17]
The story of Helga Crane, daughter of a black man and a Danish
woman whom he deserted, is obviously patterned on Larsen's
early life. Supported by a sympathetic uncle after her mother's
death, Helga grows up with all the bourgeois inclinations of the
black middle class. Deep within her, however, is a desire to
repudiate the ethic of the bourgeoisie. "The woman as bitch,"
resting latent within Helga, causes her final doom as she settles
into the "quicksand" of a mediocre domesticity. The downward,
symbolically circular path to this suffocating pit (her marriage
and the South) moves via a series of sharply etched episodes
that reveal Larsen's skill at characterization. She shows that
she is well aware of the "craft of fiction"; there is vividness,
truth (especially in her revelations of a woman's inner life),
and an ability to create scenes of encounters among people
even though she fails to be entirely convincing in her ending.
However, even Percy Lubbock, in *The Craft of Fiction*, notes
that an author may lack some part of the craft and still succeed.

Clearly, the plot is subordinate to the characterizations.
Helga Crane moves from the stultifying atmosphere of a southern
Negro college to New York, via a brief stay in Chicago where
she is scorned by her sympathetic white uncle's new wife. Thus,
rejected with finality by the American branch of her family,
Helga settles in Harlem where she finds temporary contentment.
Helga's life is a series of only evanescent fulfillments, for she
is plagued with a restlessness that has deeper causes than Miss
Larsen bothers to penetrate. It is in Harlem that Helga cultivates
and develops her "black" soul. Her embracing of this blackness
is emotionally incomplete at this juncture, however. At the
beginning of her life in Harlem she reflects:

Everything was there [in Harlem], vice and goodness, sadness and gayety, ignorance and wisdom, ugliness and beauty,
poverty and richness. And it seemed to her that somehow
of goodness, gayety, wisdom, and beauty always there was
a little more than of vice, sadness, ignorance, and ugliness.
It was only riches that did not quite transcend poverty.
'But,' said Helga Crane, 'what of that? Money isn't everything. It isn't even the half of everything. And here we have
so much else—and by ourselves. It's only outside of Harlem
among those others that money really counts for everything.'[18]

This passage foreshadows a reverse in Helga's attitude; for when
she moves from the black world into the white one of her rich
relatives in Denmark she momentarily relinquishes the moral
superiority of her black universe:

She liked it, this new life. For a time it blotted from her
mind all else. . . . To Helga Crane it was the realization of a
dream that she had dreamed persistently ever since she was
old enough to remember such vague things as day-dreams
and longings. Always she had wanted, not money, but the
things which money could give, leisure, attention, beautiful
surroundings. Things. Things. Things. (119)

Helga Crane, a nervous and somewhat complex character,
is one of the more interesting creations found in the Harlem
Renaissance novels. For one thing, she is one female of the
bourgeois who displays a desire to be sexually fulfilled. In her
decision to reject the physical and social comforts of the white
(or, as Harlem Renaissance writers termed it, Nordic) world
for the warmth and vitality of the black one, Helga fits the
Renaissance's persistent pattern. By fitting into this mold and
accepting her blackness, Helga begins to understand what moti-
vated her father's desertion:

> For the first time Helga Crane felt sympathy rather than
> contempt and hatred for that father, who so often and so
> angrily she had blamed for his desertion of her mother. She
> understood, now, his rejection, his repudiation, of the formal
> calm her mother had represented. She understood his yearn-
> ing, his intolerable need for the inexhaustible humor and the
> incessant hope of his own kind, his need for those things,
> not material, indigenous to all Negro environments. (158)

At this point Helga finds release from false values and commences
the backward journey into her true black self. She selects religion
to carry her back into the bosom of blackness. The portrait of
Helga from this point to the end becomes blurred and confus-
ing. After her "conversion," she turns to Pleasant Green, a
greasy, sweaty, mediocre preacher; despite the Oedipal impli-
cation of the search for a father, this major move is unconvincing. One explanation for the confused motivation near the end
of the book may be that she tired of writing in the midst of
describing Helga's Copenhagen experiences.[19] Suddenly, it
seems, Helga gives up living and accepts an existence that will
limp along in a wearisome, depressing manner.

The reader is left with an inkling that Larsen decided to make
Helga forget that part of her past that made her fight for the
things she wanted. The author, in an attempt to rescue herself
artistically from the book's weak ending, inserts a scene which
may provide a clue to what she intended. Helga requests a reading of Anatole France's "The Procurator of Judea." Just as
Pilate let himself forget the momentous event of his condem-
nation of Christ, so Helga, it appears, in requesting to hear this
ironic tale, seems to be telling the reader that she is simply
going to forget the past. Larsen's skillful use of this device,
however, does not compensate for the unsatisfactory religious
motivation Helga is given for becoming Mrs. Pleasant Green in
the first place.

Nella Larsen's second novel, *Passing* (1929), is written in
that hasty, seminonchalant style that put her a notch above
some of her black peers of this period in terms of simple narra-

tive technique. Therefore, even though the narrative moves
smoothly in *Passing,* the story itself is inconsequential. The
ending is melodramatic and, again (surely a Larsen weakness),
unconvincing. One is not sure whether Larsen intends the reader
to view Clare Kendry's death as suicide (intentional? accidental?)
or murder (intentional? accidental?). It is entirely possible that
she wanted this confusion to persist forever in the reader's
mind, but this certainly does not give the book any artistic
complexity that might intrigue the imagination.

One important feature of Larsen's work that is clearly evident here, as it is in *Quicksand,* is her awareness of female
sexuality. The latent desire for sexual fulfillment that Helga
satisfies with her marriage to the gross preacher is akin to Clare's
attraction to her friend's husband. In both cases, the black man
either symbolizes or brings sexual gratification, thereby reinforc-
ing the Renaissance view that it is the black, and not the white,
race that is fertile, vital, full-bodied, and rich in humaneness.

Miss Larsen never fulfilled the promise of her early successes,
and she disappeared from the literary scene after an unpleasant
exposure and accusation concerning plagiarism.[20]

A date, or time itself, perhaps, is meaningless within itself;
that added element, amplification, is needed to give significance
to a date. *The Autobiography of an Ex-Coloured Man* is a case
in point: this single novel by James Weldon Johnson was published under a pseudonym in 1912. Its inclusion in a study of
the Harlem Renaissance, however, is relevant because of its plot
and treatment of racial prejudice in a mode that parallels other
novels of this period. Moreover, its reissue in 1927 demonstrates
that Johnson's contemporaries also saw the novel as akin to
the Harlem Renaissance literature. This book forcefully upholds
the notion that Johnson can be promoted as being a precursor
of the Harlem Renaissance. The 1927 edition contained an
introduction by Johnson's good friend, Carl Van Vechten.

Despite its deceptive title, this book remains one of the most
accomplished pieces of lengthy fiction written by a Negro
during the first four decades of the twentieth century.[21] It is

a dispassionate picture of what it was like to grow up nearly
white in the racist society of the early part of this century.
The prejudice against blacks was blatantly illogical and so rampant that no excuses were needed. The protagonist of Johnson's
novel, knowing the truth of "label a mulatto white and the
world's view of him adopts the label," finally succumbs to the
advantages of uncomplicated day-to-day living as a "passer."
Even so, at the novel's end, he states: "I cannot repress the
thought that, after all, I have chosen the lesser part, that I have
sold my birthright for a mess of pottage."[22]

The melancholy of Johnson's protagonist, as well as his
cowardice, are not romantic poses. In this novel Johnson im-
plants a psychological motif which appears again and again in
the literature of the Harlem Renaissance, namely, the belief
that the Negro who abandons his people also forsakes a richness that cannot be replaced by the superficial freedom which
passing into the white world accords. This motif appeared, for
example, in nearly all of the works of Jessie Fauset, Walter
White, Claude McKay, and Nella Larsen and was certainly
implied in Rudolph Fisher's work and in Countee Cullen's
one novel.

The Autobiography of an Ex-Coloured Man is a mingling of
realism and irony. The realism is of the simplest kind: Johnson
portrays in rich, convincing detail several strata of Negro life
in the South and the East. The irony is perhaps unintentional:
the whole narrative is, first, one of understatement and, second,
one in which the hero's life changes direction radically after
one episode—the loss of money for college—which the author
intimates as being the "irony of fate."[23] Irony operates rather
successfully, too, when we realize that the hero's decision to
pass, after his seemingly objective review of both sides, fails
to give him the happiness he had expected. Dispassionate objec-
tivity may lead to nowhere, the author seems to say.

Briefly, the novel follows the life of an unnamed light-skinned
protagonist who, upon leaving the South at an early, undisclosed
age, is reared in genteel, middle-class comfort in Connecticut.
He does not discover the fact or meaning of being a Negro until
he is ten, when an embarrassing classroom situation forces this

fact upon his sensitive nature. Even then, his life is relatively
calm, and he successfully completes his adolescence, aloof from
most of his classmates but not entirely isolated. The hero, musi-
cally talented, proceeds southward to enter Atlanta University.
His money is stolen during his first day there; but rather than
explain his unhappy circumstances to the university adminis-
trators, he gives up college life and commences his life of wan-
dering and his search for self. The conflict that wars within
begins to emerge at this point: he wishes to become the best
sort of Negro, to present to the world the Negro's musical heritage, and, the easier wish to satisfy, to gratify himself as just
another man in the world, to enjoy the normal, even routine
joys experienced by the middle- or upper-middle-class white
American. As the title of the book suggests, the "hero" finally
chooses the last goal. The story follows his wanderings from
work in a cigar factory, to piano playing in a club, to travels
in Europe with his rich employer, and to the United States
again where he collects Negro folk songs. But he now abandons
his race, not simply for love of a white woman but also because
of the contradictions of his nature. On the one hand, as he
says, "I have been only a privileged spectator of their [Negroes]
inner life," and on the other, "I am possessed by a strange
longing for my mother's people."[24]

As evidenced by the society Johnson describes as well as the
duality of the protagonist's nature, the novel can be said to be
within that tradition of duality dominant in American fiction.
The tradition is clear in the protagonist's inner contradictions
and the struggles of good and evil within him, demonstrated
in his circumstances, his actions, and, most dramatically, his
inner turmoil which makes him realize that he has sold his
birthright "for a mess of pottage." This intermingling of black
and white taints the hero's moral character much as his physical
being was tainted in the belief of American society that such
an offspring, the product of racial intermingling, was a cor-
rupted version of the human species. Through the act of passing, the protagonist assumes the role of one who has failed
once again to demonstrate personal integrity. There is a continual relinquishing of values portrayed through the actions

of the protagonist; for instance, the acquiescence to the easier
way out of a dilemma (not going to college), or his lack of
shame when confronted with a lapse in his moral character
(the chasing and tormenting of a black boy from his school).
And, of course, his "passing" is his greatest act of moral cowardic
   There is a quality of the *bildungsroman* in Johnson's work,
although the forays into black propaganda and the hero's remain-
ing air of perennial questioning of his chosen path in life weaken
the impression that Johnson perceived the book on this level.
Indeed, in his autobiography he is curiously reticent about discussing his book in a literary sense and seems more concerned
with emphasizing that *The Autobiography of an Ex-Coloured
Man* was fiction rather than the story of his life.

   Although the writers of the Harlem Renaissance were not
oblivious to the influence of the black man's religion in shaping
his character, they rarely used religious settings for their novels.
The prominent exception, Countee Cullen, is not surprising,
inasmuch as he was the adopted son of a minister. Cullen's
single novel, *One Way to Heaven*, was published during the
waning days of the Harlem Renaissance (1932), but it bears
the marks of a Renaissance novel. It is, in Cullen's words, a
"two toned picture" which explores the lives of the upper and
lower strata of Negro life in Harlem during the 1920s.
   Cullen wrote to his good friend, Harold Jackman, and talked
of Flaubert: "I would give years of my life to learn to write
like that [re *Madame Bovary*].... I suppose Flaubert devoted
his entire life to mastering words and studying human emotions. Art such as his takes a life time to develop."[25] Cullen,
though never a Flaubert, achieved a polish in language and an
emotional depth in *One Way to Heaven* that clearly can be
traced to his admiration of the great masters. It is one of the
better novels of the Harlem Renaissance period.
   The novel's two stories are frequently interwoven, but it
is still primarily a novel with two different stories, one in contrast with the other because two different realms of Harlem

life are explored. Indeed, some readers may consider this narrative mode the major weakness of the novel. To be fair to Cullen,
between the significance of the title and the focusing upon
Sam Lucas at the beginning and the ending, it seems that the
Sam-Mattie love story is the primary one.

The opening scene is laid in a church where an evangelist is
speaking during a "watch meeting" night. Sam Lucas, a one-
armed con man, enters with the intention of performing his
faked act of conversion. It is the eve of a new year, with the
evangelist out to catch wayward souls and Sam Lucas out to
get the most out of his highly practiced art. He strides to the
altar and presents his razor and cards as symbols of his conversion. A young lady in the audience, moved by his action, submits to the "spirit" and is truly converted. Thus, their relationship starts on a compromised basis because of his deceit and
her subsequent naïveté in believing that religion, which has
brought them together, will shape their future life together.
They marry, although Sam encounters difficulties unknown
to him before in the wooing and winning of Mattie. This is
evident in the following scene, which also serves to illustrate
the sacred and profane aspects that form a leitmotif in the
novel:

> They walked along in a silence which was mainly fear of
> themselves, fear of the fierce desires at the roots of their
> beings. . . . Sam had forgotten the services of the church as
> soon and as lightly as he had stepped across its threshold
> out into the sharp January sun. All that he was concerned
> with now was the woman at his side. . . . He wished he knew
> how to tackle her; for he felt that she was like some new and
> strange being, unlike the other women he had known. Those
> others had been like himself, creatures of action and not of
> speech. . . . He knew when a flippant word meant 'Leave
> me be.' But this girl . . . She seemed near at hand, as close
> as if they were linked together by a strip of flesh, yet in-

accessible, as if getting religion and joining church had
suddenly grown walls about her and shut her away from
the world. Her eyes smiled at him, but their message was . . .
'Speak to me' and 'Tell me things.' The palm of his hand was
moist with panic.[26]

After marrying, Sam has a hard time keeping up the deception
about his new-found religion. He cheats on Mattie, moves out
to be with his woman, but returns to Mattie in the end when
he is suffering from pneumonia. Just before he dies, he pretends
to believe again and Mattie is happy. Cullen suggests that Sam's
last act of deception secures his salvation because it is sacrificial.
    Mattie is employed as a maid for the Harlem socialite
Constancia Brandon, a witty, pretentious, and extravagant
woman who mocks as she is mocked. The sycophants who
hang about her salon are much more savagely portrayed because they are unaware of the fragility and senselessness of the
putative Negro "society." Constancia is well aware of the cracks
in the Negro psyche, but she possesses, in addition to intelligence (she is a Radcliffe graduate), common sense and a love
for those Negro strengths and unique qualities that enrich life.
(The truth or falsity of this premise is not the point, either in
this novel or in any of the others that promote the idea of black
vitality.) At one point, Constancia states:

> I often think the Negro is God Almighty's one mistake, but
> as I look about me at white people, I am forced to say so
> are we all. It isn't being colored that annoys me. I could go
> white if I wanted to, but I am too much of a hedonist; I
> enjoy life too much, and enjoyment isn't across the line.
> Money is there, and privilege, and the sort of power which
> comes with numbers; but as for enjoyment, they don't know
> what it is. (187)

As viewed through Constancia, then, blacks are implied to
be basically superior to whites in terms of warmth, compassion,
humaneness, and ability to enjoy life despite social restrictions and

persecution. It is obvious, also, that Cullen admired his Constancia: she outshines Mattie and Sam so outrageously that the reader is left wishing that Cullen had written two books instead of one.

The desire to portray all strata of Harlem social classes weakens the book because the characterizations never achieve full dimensions. The failure to present Harlem in depth is a pity, for one is struck by Cullen's facility with language in his descriptive or narrative passages. His dialogue is natural, too, even though it seems forced in some of the scenes with Constancia. On a deeper level, Cullen demonstrates an awareness of the uses of symbol and metaphor, and he displays a feeling for the sort of literary complexity absent in some of the other Harlem Renaissance novels.

The symbols of the razor and cards, pervasive throughout the book, are manifestations of the evil that Sam professes to have abandoned. The salvation theme is also developed through the symbols of cards and razor and concurrently through the use of dark and light imagery and colors. For instance, red has the dual symbolism of salvation and sin (e.g., the "blood of the Lamb" and red lips). In the case of the red kimona that Sam offers Mattie, the color reflects the shame Mattie shares in joining with Sam, the overt sinner. White functions in the traditional mode to symbolize purity, but black is employed to epitomize beauty instead of dark deeds and foul acts.

Like the razor, Sam, too, is an instrument: he is an instrument of salvation. Heaven has sent Sam to Mattie and she reclaims him for this divine abode. Sam is an instrument of salvation because his final act is presented ultimately as an act of sacrifice rather than of pure chicanery. Without Sam's ruse Mattie would be doomed; she would be barred from the salvation she earnestly seeks.

If there is a single metaphor for Cullen's book it lies in the title: one way to get into heaven is through a type of personal salvation that results from well-meaning deception. Mattie is fooled by the pretense, the "trickster" act of Sam, but Sam, in a roundabout, theological sense, is possibly saved as well. He pretends to hear music and to see bright lights in order to convince Mattie that he has had a vision. Before he dies, "he could feel Mattie's hand tremble on his forehead. Aunt Mandy stood transfixed and mute. He knew that for them he was forever saved" (279). Thus, with careful attention to the details of Sam's vision, Cullen brings to an orderly conclusion the chaos of troubled souls. The fact that Cullen begins and concludes his work with the lives of Sam and Mattie is evidence that they were meant to be the primary focus of Cullen's story. Therefore, Cullen should have concentrated on it. The novel would have been strenghtened by greater attention to these confused, common folk, especially since it is their story that supplies the novel with its thematic title.

It was another poet, the most enduring and well-known survivor of the Harlem Renaissance, who wrote perhaps the most appealing and least controversial novel during the waning of the Renaissance. It was during his student days (in his mid-twenties, however) at Lincoln University that Langston Hughes started writing his first novel, *Not Without Laughter* (1930). Although the book was favorably reviewed, Hughes later expressed disappointment with his character portrayals. Here he was perhaps not the best judge, for his characterizations are one of the strengths of this frankly nostalgic novel. Despite weaknesses in the structure and an obvious simplicity in Hughes's interpretation of the lives he describes, the book was warmly applauded by some reviewers whose opinions are worth quoting:

> It is written with understanding, tolerance and beauty, it lays special claim to the attention of those who love life and its mirroring in fiction.[27]

> It is significant because even where it fails, it fails beautifully, and where it succeeds—namely, in its intimate characterizations and in its local color and charm—it succeeds where almost all others have failed.[28]

> Its strength lies in this simplicity, in its author's unflinching honesty, and in his ability to make the reader feel very deeply the problems of his characters.[29]

Even Martha Gruening, in her article berating the writers of
the Harlem Renaissance, gives tribute to Hughes:

> [It] is not only uniquely moving and lovely among Negro
> novels but among books written about America. It is affirma-
> tive in a sense in which no other book by an American Negro
> is, for it is the story of a Negro happily identified with his
> own group, who because of his identification tells what is
> essentially, despite the handicaps of poverty and prejudice,
> the story of a happy childhood.[30]

Hughes explains what he was attempting to do in *Not Without Laughter* in his autobiography:

> I wanted to write about a typical Negro family in the Middle
> West, about people like those I had known in Kansas. But I
> thought I had been a typical Negro boy. . . . We [his family]
> were poor—but different. For purposes of the novel, how-
> ever, I created around myself what seemed to me a family
> more typical of Negro life in Kansas than my own had been.[31]

Reality through nostalgia was a primary concern, then; and to
treat the novel as one with a complex theme and motive is to
do the book an injustice.

The story centers on the life of Sandy as he grows up in a
small town in Kansas (Stanton). His mother, Annjee, is married
to a no-account, good-looking mulatto named Jimboy. Annjee's
mother, Aunt Hager, a version of the mammy prototype, says
of him: "Who ever heard of a nigger named Jimboy, anyhow?
Next place, I ain't never seen a yaller dude yet that meant a
dark woman no good—an' Annjee is dark!"[32]

Sandy has two aunts, Tempy and Harriett. Tempy has risen
in the world and has all the shallow veneer of the "nouveau
bourgeois." In reality, she is unsure of herself, although she
makes it clear how she is to be treated and, in receiving this
phony respect, remains isolated from her warm-hearted, unpretentious family. Tempy and others in her "class" know how
tenuous their role is, for they "were all people of standing in

the darker world—doctors, school-teachers, a dentist, a lawyer, a hairdresser. . . . One's family as a topic of conversation, however, was not popular in high circles, for too many of Stanton's dark society folks had sprung from humble family trees and low black bottoms" (256).

Sandy's other aunt, Harriett, epitomizes the uninhibited, sensuous, generous woman—the sort of person, as Hughes says, who never "soiled" her mind by too much thinking. She hates the stultifying atmosphere of her home because Aunt Hager is obsessed by religion and its sometime by-product, sin. Harriett displays toward her mother an impatience that erupts in venomous verbal spats. At one point she tells Aunt Hager:

> I don't want to be respectable if I have to be stuck up and dicty like Tempy is. . . . She's colored and I'm colored and I haven't seen her since before Easter. . . . It's not being black that matters with her, though, it's being poor, and that's what we are, you and me and Annjee, working for white folks and washing clothes and going in back doors, and taking tips and insults. I'm tired of it, mama, I want to have a good time once in a while. (45)

Later, she shouts this shocking statement to her mother: "Your old Jesus is white, I guess, that's why! He's white and stiff and don't like niggers!" (45).

In the end it is Harriett (by this time a night club singer) who intercedes in Sandy's behalf to aid him in the first steps towards achieving both his and Aunt Hager's dream of completing his schooling. Sandy's mother is not enthusiastic about education for the boy; work that pays enough to keep one alive is all that she considers necessary. But Harriett, even though rejecting Aunt Hager's way of life for herself, reminds Annjee, "Why, Aunt Hager'd turn over in her grave if she heard you talking so calmly about Sandy leaving school—the way she wanted to make something out of this kid" (322).

The fictional canvas is rich in characterization and in its portrayal of a racial milieu little known at that time in our social history. The style of Hughes's prose is unrestrained and casual, tinged at times with an air of nostalgia and naïveté. The book is weakened by its episodic structure and by its incomplete, faltering characterization of the protagonist, Sandy. The novel sometimes seems to be more a novel about Aunt Hager, for she overwhelms the imagination and is presented in full dimension. Still, Hughes dissected "the ways of black folk" with a skill that he, and others, underestimated. In choosing the mode of the realistic novel, in fusing it with the ambiance of the black folk tradition, Hughes wrote a book that is as charming as it is honest.

NOTES

1. Countee Cullen, *On These I Stand* (New York: Harper & Row, 1947), pp. 25-26.

2. Augusta V. Jackson, "The Renascence of Negro Literature, 1922 to 1929" (M.A. thesis, Atlanta University, 1926), p. 141.

3. For some reason, one or two references imply that Merrit is a doctor (e.g., Nick Aaron Ford, in his book *The Contemporary Negro Novel: A Study in Race Relations* (Boston: Mesdor Publishing Co., 1936).

4. Rudolph Fisher, *The Walls of Jericho* (New York: Knopf, 1928), p. 37. All subsequent quotes will have page numbers included in the text in parentheses.

5. John Louis Clarke, "Mystery Novel Writer Is Interviewed over the Radio," *Pittsburgh Courier*, 21 January 1933.

6. Ibid.

7. Ibid.

8. *New York Herald Tribune*, 24 May 1948.

9. Claude McKay, "A Negro to His Critics," *New York Herald Tribune Books*, 6 March 1932, p. 1.

10. Claude McKay, *A Long Way from Home* (New York: Harcourt, c. 1970, c. 1937), p. 245.

11. McKay was quite a few years older than Hughes, Cullen, Thurman, Larsen, and Hurston, for instance. He found himself between this group and the elder statesmen of the Harlem Renaissance (e.g., J. W. Johnson, DuBois, Locke).

12. McKay, *A Long Way from Home*, pp. 282-283.

13. Claude McKay, *Banjo* (New York: Harper, 1929), p. 200.

14. Kenneth Ramchard, *The West Indian Novel and Its Background* (New York: Barnes and Noble, 1970), p. 259.

15. Stephen H. Bronz, *Roots of Negro Racial Consciousness; the 1920's: Three Harlem Renaissance Authors* (New York: Libra Publishers, 1964), p. 89.

16. Robert A. Bone, *The Negro Novel in America* (New Haven: Yale University Press, c. 1965), p. 97.

17. Ibid., p. 103.

18. Nella Larsen, *Quicksand* (New York: Macmillan, c. 1971, c. 1928), pp. 88-89. All subsequent quotes will have page numbers included in the text in parentheses.

19. Larsen communicated this weariness to Carl Van Vechten in a letter with an envelope postmarked 7 December 1926 (Beinecke Library, Yale University, Nella Larsen Imes file).

20. Larsen, *Quicksand*, p. 16 ["Introduction"].

21. Johnson, in his autobiography *Along This Way*, wrote that "The Chameleon" had been suggested as a title, and he was not sure that he had been wise in rejecting it.

22. James Weldon Johnson, *The Autobiography of an Ex-Coloured Man* (New York: A. A. Knopf, 1961, c. 1955), p. 211.

23. The phrase "irony of fate," despite Fowler's dismissal of it, certainly is valid, at least for referring to works that appear to employ this notion. Another instance of its use in this novel is the lynching scene which triggers the hero's decision to pass.

24. Johnson, *The Autobiography of an Ex-Coloured Man*, p. 210.

25. Countee Cullen to Harold Jackman, 1 July 1923 (Beinecke Library, Yale University).

26. Countee Cullen, *One Way to Heaven* (New York: Harper, 1932), pp. 82-83. All subsequent quotes will have page numbers included in the text in parentheses.

27. *New York Herald Tribune Books*, 27 July 1930, p. 5.

28. *The Nation* 131 (6 August 1930): 157.

29. *Saturday Review* 7 (23 August 1930): 69.

30. Martha Gruening, "The Negro Renaissance," *Hound and Horn* 5 (April-June 1932): 508.

31. Langston Hughes, *The Big Sea* (New York: Hill and Wang, 1963, c. 1940), pp. 303-304. Hughes's family was atypically professional.

32. Langston Hughes, *Not Without Laughter* (New York: Knopf, 1930), p. 18. All subsequent quotes will have page numbers included in the text in parentheses.

six

THE MINOR NOVELS

A second string of writers, the minor novelists, were an integral part of the Harlem Renaissance movement in a personal as well as in a literary sense. Wallace Thurman, Walter White, Jessie Fauset, W.E.B. DuBois, George Schuyler, and Arna Bontemps are the minor novelists who, though not first rate, are in the mainstream of the Renaissance in scope and theme.

Wallace Thurman was "perhaps the most symbolic figure of the Literary Renaissance in Harlem."[1] He was far removed from the propagandistic fiction of DuBois, but this fact didn't make Thurman the better novelist. Unfortunately, the intensity of his desire to become a true artist was frustrated by his inability to create convincing fictional characters. A parallel weakness was his failure to produce a world that illuminated his experiences among the Harlem literati; he succeeded in producing only a caricature.

In a newspaper article sketch of Wallace Thurman, it was written: "His pet hates . . . are all Negro uplift societies, Greta Garbo, Negro novelists including himself, Negro society, NYS divorce laws, morals, religion, politics, censors, policemen, sympathetic white folks who go in for helping Negroes and . . . every damned spot in the United States except Manhattan."[2] This description, though mocking, captures some of the contradictory nature of Thurman and hints at his predilection for hating. Those who need love the most sometimes exceed in exhibiting the emotion of hate; Thurman was apparently such a person.

There is a Negro folk saying, "The blacker the berry, the sweeter the juice," which Thurman used ironically for the title of his first novel, *The Blacker the Berry* (1929). It is a woeful tale of color prejudice told from all angles, the tale of a victim who acquiesces in the belief that her black skin is, indeed, a horrible affliction which must be eradicated. The heroine, Emma Lou, is tortured like the damned; she suffers rejection by her color-conscious family and later by her black business employers, ridicule by her classmates and insensitive passersby on the streets of Harlem, and sexual exploitation by a mulatto who has no real love for her but is willing to give her the attention she craves. Thurman rather unrealistically forces Emma Lou to accept her undesirability, even though time and again she is well able to function in ordinary situations (e.g., school, work) skillfully. His unabating imposition of the corrosive effects of unthinking prejudice lessens the effect of Emma Lou's realization that her only freedom lies in her acceptance of her blackness. In addition to its weak psychology, *The Blacker the Berry* is poorly written and ineptly constructed. Generally, it may be said that Thurman, despite his admiration of James and Tolstoy, never learned enough about the art of fiction to produce a first-rate novel.

Thurman's second and more interesting book, *Infants of the Spring* (1932), suffers from some of the same weaknesses as his first novel: a misuse of the elements of satire; an inability to dramatize a situation successfully; an excessive use of conversation to feed information about his pet hates; and a plethora of characters in the *roman à clef* tradition—the latter including Tony Crews (representing Langston Hughes), DeWitt Clinton (Countee Cullen), Dr. Parkes (Alain Locke), Dr. Manfred Trout (Rudolph Fisher), and Sweetie May Carr (Zora Neale Hurston).

Infants of the Spring, however, is one of the more entertaining novels to emerge from the Harlem Renaissance literary period. Thurman makes use of his character Raymond Taylor in the same manner McKay used Ray in his novels—to criticize and examine this extraordinary time in which the black writer, for better or for worse, was being recognized by the literary establishment. Thurman's conclusions were bitter, even carping. He seemed to complain acidly, as Harold Cruse did thirty-five years later in *The Crisis of the Negro Intellectual,* that the Harlem Renaissance movement was aimless and had too many people who were poseurs instead of capable producers of great literature. The black writers and artists of the period were gradually aware that they were indeed part of a movement. Their efforts to give shape to it, however, were thwarted by a conflict between individual aims and desires, headiness from excessive praise and recognition, and a disinclination to make a concerted attack on the problem of being a black artist seeking a spiritual connection with Black Africa while living and participating in a Western culture.

Thurman was too close to the Harlem Renaissance in both time and sentiment to ridicule it effectively; hence, such an attempt fails in the *Infants of the Spring.* In turning his back on the movement that had quickened his creative energy, Thurman focused his disappointed spirit and sense of rejection on this unevenly written, almost psychotic novel. There is a vividness, however, that his first book lacked. Too, as is true in all caricature, there was an element of truth in his exaggerated characterizations. Langston Hughes found *Infants of the Spring* "a compelling book," but he must have viewed it much as a

family looking at home movies: no matter how poor the pictures, the scenes and persons are enjoyed because of familiarity
and personal interest. Hughes, in a further discussion of Thurman
wrote:

> But none of these things [his books, his brilliance] pleased
> Wallace Thurman. He wanted to be a *very* good writer, like
> Gorki or Thomas Mann, and he felt that he was merely a
> journalistic writer. His critical mind, comparing his pages
> to the thousands of other pages he had read, by Proust,
> Melville, Tolstoy, Galsworthy, Dostoevski, Henry James,
> Sainte-Beauve, Taine, Anatole France, found his own pages
> vastly wanting. So he contented himself by writing a great
> deal for money, laughing bitterly at his fabulously concocted
> "true stories," creating two bad motion pictures of the
> "Adults Only" type for Hollywood, drinking more and more
> gin, and then threatening to jump out of windows at people's
> parties and kill himself.[3]

With all of its faults, *Infants of the Spring* is valuable, for it
chronicles some of the more extreme moments of the Harlem
Renaissance period. It ought to be read with an awareness of
its hyperbolic quality. It is a novel which relies heavily on
characterization (not fully portrayed, however) and on episodic
glimpses into one manner of life (the bohemian) that added
zest to the Harlem scene during the 1920s. The setting is Niggeratti Manor, a large house partitioned into apartments or small
studios for Negro artists. The owner, Euphoria Blake, believes
in the necessity of communication, companionship, and "Art"
for the advancement of the Negro in American society. When
her place begins to look and sound more like a bawdy house,
Euphoria tells her undisciplined tenants they must leave and
she closes Niggeratti Manor. Between the opening and closing
of this artistic haven, the reader is introduced to various types
of writers and artists who do more talking than work. None

of the characters is especially memorable; even Raymond Taylor (presumably the author's voice), the protagonist, is weakly depicted. At the novel's dénouement, Taylor is at loose ends and other characters face rather gloomy personal problems with no hint of resolution in sight. Nothing seems to have achieved meaning; but it is a nihilism that is utterly uninstructive. The book's end in despair and disillusionment coincides with Thurman's personal viewpoint, but the end seems to be one concocted for effect rather than one that grows from the actions in the central portion of the book.

Thurman is credited with half-authorship of a third novel, *The Interne* (1932), coauthored with L. Furman. This, too, is a poorly constructed book. Moreover, it is so rife with the worst examples of fictive writing that nothing can be said in its favor. Some have speculated that Thurman did not write any part of the book, but there is evidence in some of Thurman's correspondence that he actually collaborated with Furman on this exaggerated, melodramatic novel. The ironic and sad part about *The Interne* is that the novel depicted a horribly run hospital—the sort of hospital in which Thurman died in 1934. It is not inconceivable that Thurman saw the irony of the whole thing, too, as he lay dying of tuberculosis one cold December day on Welfare Island.

Walter White's first book, *Fire in the Flint* (1924), is more of a propagandistic tract against lynching and Southern denigration of blacks than a novel. "All art is propaganda," said DuBois, and Walter White was undoubtedly a proponent of this idea.

It is not, however, a dismissal to call White's book a tract rather than a novel. He was not a novelist by profession, and, although he was pleased by the somewhat favorable reception given the book, he exhibited no strong, driving force to pursue a literary career. *Fire in the Flint* is the story of an intelligent (yet naive) Negro doctor who returns to his home in the South to practice medicine. But the "hero," Kenneth Harper, is almost obtuse in his belief that he can be objective about the race problem while living in a Georgia town. Here is one of his musings:

The proscriptions which he and others of his race were forced to endure were inconvenient, yet they were apparently a part of life, one of its annoyances, a thing which had always been and probably would be for all time to come. Therefore, he reasoned, why bother with it any more than one was forced to by sheer necessity?[4]

It takes the brutal force of an attack on himself, after having suffered through the knowledge of the rape of his sister and lynching of his brother, to force him to recognize that passivity cannot help the Negro, that the plight of the Negro is uniquely real and terrible, equally demoralizing to both races.

Some of the tension of the physical and moral entrapment of the educated black in the small Southern town is revealed in *Fire in the Flint.* The overall authenticity of this portrait is a positive feature of the novel. And the outrageous final scene, despite its fierce melodrama, is powerful in its appeal to the decent person's moral conscience.

Walter White wrote one more novel before giving up fiction for his more effective work with the National Association for the Advancement of Colored People. *Flight* (1926) is also a study of the black bourgeoisie, and it contains one element that reappears thematically in Negro novels of this period: passing. This book is essentially a history of the life of Mimi Daquin, a light-skinned Creole, from her earliest days through her flight from the stuffy black society of Atlanta to the East where she eventually passes into the white world. Just as in other books of this type, especially the novels of Jessie Fauset, Mimi ultimately returns to the black world because she senses a barrenness in the white one. After a secret visit to Harlem, Mimi reflects: "She felt within her a renewing of her old eagerness towards life. Here was something real that the unknowing and unseeing had called 'native humour' and 'Negro comedy.' But, somewhat vaguely, she felt the thing went deeper than that."[5] It was reunification with the true black soul, of course, and Mimi, like many who followed her, made her flight back into the bosom of the collective racial family.

In a functional sense, Jessie Fauset's greatest contributions
to the Harlem Renaissance were her position as literary editor
of *The Crisis* and the warm encouragement she gave to younger
writers. Fauset, true to the false modesty of the sedate bourgeois, never revealed her age, but she was closer to McKay than
to Cullen or Hughes inasmuch as she graduated from Cornell
in 1905. She attended the University of Pennsylvania where
she received an M.A. degree in French; later she studied at the
Sorbonne. Before and after her editorial work at *The Crisis*,
she taught in high schools in Washington, D.C., and the Bronx.

Fauset wrote about the black bourgeoisie, and the individuals
whom she depicted were the tormented ones, shackled or restrained by the folly of racial prejudice. We are presented with
blacks who are educated, refined, and sensitive to the bipolar
racial world. We have a wide array, then, of perceptive Negroes
living with *angst* in an antagonistic environment. This is the
circumscribed world Fauset describes with more sincerity than
skill. She never really learned to control the tools of fiction,
but this failure never kept her editors from publishing her work.
In her time, then, she was not a neglected author.

Jessie Fauset knew nearly everyone who had any artistic
leaning during the Harlem Renaissance period. She opened
her home to young Negro artists but was cautious about invit-
ing curious whites, according to Langston Hughes. Claude
McKay wrote of her: "Miss Fauset is prim and dainty as a prim-
rose, and her novels are quite as fastidious and precious."[6]
While he did not intend this comment to be slurring, artistically
its effect is close to devastating. Her style is indeed "fastidious"
to the point that her prose is vitiated by her excessively careful
attention to defining her characters (always worthy) and the
shameless way in which they are treated in a symbolically anti-
podean world. There is, then, a sterility in her style. If she was,
as William Stanley Braithwaite panegyrically wrote, "the potential Jane Austen of Negro literature,"[7] she missed by a wide
mark in characterization and stylistic exposition. Whereas
Jane Austen was unquestionably an artist of characterization,

a forte revealed, in part, through a masterful control of speech, Jessie Fauset was unable to create characters who possessed any dimensions in their personalities.

The novels of Jessie Fauset span the years 1924-1933, commencing with *There Is Confusion.* In this novel we are introduced to the thematic format that is repeated in most of her subsequent novels: educated blacks in the hostile, unfair world; the schizophrenia of the rejected mulatto who finally passes; the color caste system among Negroes; and the existence of an ancestral past within Negro society that is as complex as that existing in the white world. Fauset usually gives her Negroes (the "better" ones) a family background that is undeniably respectable. This is her way of attempting to create a symbolic tension that is, in reality, lacking in her novels.

In *There Is Confusion,* the heroine, Joanna Marshall, seeks recognition as an artist. Although she attains a measure of success, she gives it up for marriage to the one man she has always loved (and, surely to the exasperation of the reader, he is a man blessed with the sort of patience that only a romantic female novelist could create).

When a reader is faced with a Jessie Fauset novel, what is to be expected in terms of literary style and novelistic technique? *There Is Confusion* gives the reader examples of some characteristic failures Fauset was unable to transcend: stiff, self-conscious narration, overuse of coincidence, faulty characterization, and unrealistic dialogue. The latter weakness is particularly noticeable, as in the following example:

'*Love* is our refuge and strength.'

He kissed her reverently. 'Yes, thank God, we've got Love. That is the great compensation. We've tried everything else, dear: you, your career; and I, my self-indulgence. And we've found what we wanted was each other. But you're right, Joanna, it is frightful to see the havoc that this queer bugaboo of color works among us. . . . '

'*Entbehren, sollst du,*' Joanna quoted. 'If you're black in
America, you have to renounce. But that's life, too, Peter.
You've got to renounce something—always.'
'I'm afraid you'll have to give up your career, dear Joanna——'
'Of course, of course, I know it.'
'For, if there should be children, I want, Oh, Joanna, I hope——'
'You want them to be different from both you and me,
Peter.'
'Not so different from you. You were always so brave, so
plucky. But, Joanna, if they are like me they'll have so much
to fight, and they'll need you to help them.'
'We can do anything together, Peter.'[8]

   Fauset's second novel, *Plum Bun* (1929), does show more
control of plot, and the story itself is more interesting. Some
of the incidents and characters parallel actual facts and persons
of the period (the rejection of the black sculptor, Augusta
Savage, for study at Fontainebleau, the characters Van Meier
[DuBois?] and the Sandburgs [the Van Vechtens?]); the
impression is one of greater immediacy and importance. The
whole spectrum of passing is examined. The theme of the
acceptance of one's race and black culture reflects Fauset's
major concern in fictive writing.
   Chinaberry Tree (1931) is a curious novel that is weakened
by the author's avowed desire to "have depicted something of
the homelife of the colored American who is not being pressed
too hard by the Furies of Prejudice, Ignorance, and Economic
Injustice. And behold he is not so vastly different from any
other American, just distinctive."[9] Unfortunately, Fauset made
them distinctively boring; moreover, as a controlling symbol,
the chinaberry tree is lacking in any deep significance.
   By the time Fauset published her last novel, *Comedy:
American Style* (1933), the vestiges of the Harlem Renaissance were few, and the world in general was in an economic,
moral, and psychological slump. Perhaps this accounts for the
hysterical characterization of the heroine, Olivia Cary. In any

case, the novel is unsuccessful because its presentation of a madly color-conscious woman becomes a caricature. The tone of the novel is strident and there are incidents that are unbelievable. In this book, more than in her others, Fauset portrays another of her weak, uncomplaining male characters. Dr. Cary is byond belief, however, and this is just one of several weaknesses that obscure the seriousness of Fauset's concern about prejudice and its effects.

What, then, did Jessie Fauset contribute to black literature and to the Harlem Renaissance? What were her strengths and weaknesses? Despite her most obvious deficiencies—poor plotting and characterization, banal romanticism, weak dialogue— there are some positive qualities in her work that make it necessary to include her in a survey of the literature of this period: there was the cumulative effect of her concentration upon certain themes (the consequences of prejudice, both against Negroes and among Negroes, the value of the Negro's racial heritage, and the ubiquitous theme of passing). She managed to bring before the reading public a view of a genuine milieu of Negro society that whites rarely saw or knew existed. If the propaganda novel has any legitimacy (and it has not been altogether shunned in the United States), Fauset's books can be said to have value in their promotion of fairness to the black race. In an interview Miss Fauset once said:

> Life is hard for everyone, but to ordinary difficulties are added intangible difficulties in the case of the Negro. For him life is very uncertain. He's never sure what sort of a break he may get. Looking at the matter dispassionately, it would seem as though my people are cut off from advantages exactly in proportion to their color.[10]

In order to disclose, in dramatic form, the difficulties and the compensations of being black in twentieth-century America, Fauset chose the novel as her weapon of enlightenment. That she succeeded as well as she did is one more curious but not wholly displeasing fact in American literary history. The value of the function she served may be disputed; the truth of it, the function itself, may not. Careers have soared and have been influential on the basis of less substantial performances.

W. E. B. DuBois, like Walter White, was not a novelist; rather, he was a writer who wrote some novels. His novels, as DuBois freely admitted, were propaganda for his vast reservoir of ideas concerning "The Race" and adjunctive concepts such as Pan-Africanism and socialism. During the height of the Harlem Renaissance, DuBois's second novel, *Dark Princess* (1928), was published. It was in this book that he was able to give free rein to his belief that the dark peoples of the world should unite in order to strengthen their advance into the mainstream of civilization. The novel is overburdened with plot and counter-plot, although the central character, Matthew Towns, never loses his importance as the protagonist. Towns, for all the prominence DuBois gives him, never comes across as a real person, fully developed or more than one-dimensional. After leaving medical school in anger because he is not permitted to do obstetrical practice in a white hospital, Towns goes to Berlin where he meets Kautilya, an Indian princess. Kautilya is deeply committed to unification of the dark peoples of the world and urges the unnamed organization, formed for this purpose, to let Towns work for it in the United States. Towns's career in this work is short-lived and he ends up in jail because of his connection with a terrorist within the organization. At this point, he turns from world unity to black politics in Chicago. But DuBois is really interested in the dark people's unification idea and maneuvers Towns back to this interest and back into the arms of Kautilya whom he has always loved. The whole story serves as a vehicle for DuBois to express his sentiments about the necessity for international cohesiveness among the darker races and to reveal the shallowness and corruption of political life in the United States. The combination of these two problematic topics is simply too much for one novel, how-

ever. DuBois was not helped by his florid, ultraromantic style
that turgidly burdened what often reads more like a polemical
treatise than a novel. The book, of course, is significant for
giving us a better understanding of DuBois. It is also a notable
example of what many blacks thought ought to be written—
a tale with an obvious moral, one that reveals the social injustices
suffered by blacks, a dramatic rendition of middle-class blacks
fighting for selfhood and manhood in a compromised world.

George Schuyler's *Black No More* (1931) is a strong attempt
to produce an unadulterated satire. The obvious thrust for
humor at the expense of untenable ideas and people is carried
beyond the bounds of effective satire, however. This defect
weakens the important underlying thesis of the novel, i.e., the
absurdity of color prejudice. Whereas the author fails in satire,
he succeeds in comedy, although it may appear to be low and
broad. Subtlety, however, is not Mr. Schuyler's avowed purpose.

Before examining the novel, it may be useful to explore the
author and his ideas about black and white, and black art, in
particular. Schuyler's expressed ideas are paramount in importance if one is to appreciate the full meaning of *Black No More*.

In one issue of *The Nation,* that which preceded the issue
containing Langston Hughes's "The Negro Artist and the Racial
Mountain," Schuyler wrote about what he labeled "The Negro-
Art Hokum."[11] He commenced his thesis with the lines: "Negro
art 'made in America' is non-existent as the widely advertised
profundity of Cal Coolidge. . . . Negro art there has been, is,
and will be among the numerous black nations of Africa; but
to suggest the possibility of any such development among the
ten million colored people in this republic is self-evident foolishness."[12] Although Schuyler acknowledges the "racial" origins
of spirituals and jazz, he discredits the idea that these genres
are exclusively Negro: "They are no more expressive or char-

acteristic of the Negro race than the music and dancing of the
Appalachian highlanders or the Dalmation peasantry are expressive or characteristic of the Caucasian race."[13] In his novel,
Schuyler supports his thesis that the Negro is a darker image
of the white: as soon as his "hero" turns white, there is nothing
in his voice, mode of speech, his walk, or his attitudes that
might betray his black heritage. In his essay Schuyler also
states, "Aside from his color, which ranges from very dark
brown to pink, your American Negro is just plain American."[14]
Since the black man is nothing but a darker version of the white
race, "how, then, can the black American be expected to produce art and literature dissimilar to that of the white American?"[15]
Indeed, according to Schuyler, he does not.

This is the sort of philosophy that gave birth to the sincere
if misfired satire, *Black No More*.[16] Although distortion is the
basic technique of satire, Schuyler displays a lack of balance
in his portrayals of deluded characters. The story, briefly,
follows the life and career of Matthew Fisher who, undergoing
the whitening process of one Dr. Crookman, becomes the white
man, Max Disher. He then journeys to Atlanta to look for a
white girl who had refused to dance with him in a Harlem cabaret
when he had been Matthew Fisher. He finds the girl, marries
her, and becomes a leader in her father's antiblack organization
(patterned on the KKK), the "Knights of Nordica." Eventually,
so many people turn white that the country goes wild in its
efforts to insure racial identity. In the end, the mark of exclusive-
ness is to have skin which is tinted brown, thus repudiating
whiteness and, it is hoped, proving the foolishness of the notion
that one's worth is based on skin color. The final point is not
as convincing as the author might have wished, for we cannot
be sure that he has accomplished anything more than to poke
fun at people and organizations he did not like (e.g., W. E. B.
DuBois, the NAACP, the KKK). Perhaps the most odious
notions in the novel, stretched out to metaphoric dimensions,
are the desire of Max for "the shimmering strawberry blond"

from Georgia and his happiness and satisfaction with her after
his transformation from black to white.

It is difficult to equate Matthew Fisher's desire for "the
shimmering strawberry blond" as the natural lust of male for
female because his friend, Bunny, reminds him early in the
book, "Ever' gal I ever seen you with looked like an ofay" (19).
Matthew's penchant for light-skinned women lessens the impact
of his successful interest in the blond and adds more crudity
than profundity to this quasi-satire. Schuyler shifts inconsistently
back and forth between his thesis of black as dark-white and
black as something different. The weight, of course, is on the
former, especially when the newly white hero muses, "As a boy
he had been taught to look up to white folks as just a little less
than gods; now he found them little different from the Negroes,
except that they were uniformly less courteous and less interesting" (63). Schuyler's main concern, in any case, was to reveal
the fatuousness of both races, to demonstrate that both were
vain and silly about race, that black and white were twins facing
the same problems in much the same manner.

Northrop Frye states: "Two things are essential to satire.
One is wit or humour, the other an object of attack."[17] Since
Black No More certainly has an object, even though it lacks
much of wit, we cannot dismiss the book entirely; racial prejudice
is attacked with savagery and sexual myths are largely discredited.
The distortion that grows out of the action and the minimal
characterization (granted, less important in satire) do save
Schuyler from failing totally in what Rudolph Fisher correctly
labeled a novel which is "primarily sociological, not primarily
literary."[18]

During the 1920s Arna Bontemps was chiefly a poet. His
first novel, *God Sends Sunday,* was published in 1931 and therefore rests in that period of the Harlem Renaissance that one
could easily call "the expiring moment." Robert A. Bone is
correct when he states that the book "is an unadulterated

product of the Negro Renaissance."[19] The novel is one of the few during this period to deal exclusively with the lower-class Negro. Certainly it is unique because of its author's total absorption in the low-bred milieu which he depicts. McKay and Fisher gave black literature common types, but the Banjos and Shines of their novels offered contrasts and (sometimes) comic relief for the intellectuals who served as spokesmen for the authors. But in *God Sends Sunday*, the action is centered on the fame, fortune, and disintegration of the likable hero, Little Augie.

There is not a great deal of action, the main emphasis being on characterization. The author focuses on Little Augie's vision of life and the social relationships that give meaning to his non-reflective personality. From the beginning there is an indication that the use of black superstition and motif will play a small but important role in the story's development. When Little Augie was born, for instance, there was a caul over his face and "due to [this] mysterious veil with which he had entered the world" he was considered lucky.[20] Although this caul signifies special eminence for Little Augie, it also, in a strong psychological manner, separates him from those about him.[21] Therefore, his youthful departure from the surroundings of his earliest years is predictable.

The story is a graceful rendering of Little Augie's life from his beginnings as "a thin, undersized boy" to his late middle age when he appears as "a tiny withered man in a frayed and ancient Prince Albert and a badly battered silk hat" (3, 122). The tale, then, charts the ascent and descent of one man's life. At the height of his career as a jockey, Little Augie represents the swaggering, happy-go-lucky Negro one encounters in some of the works by Fisher, Hughes, and McKay. Little Augie is a vagabond who takes chances and tempts fate. When his luck is good and he is riding high, he lives extravagantly, expansively, in a colorful and gaudy fashion. It is an elemental world that Little Augie inhabits: one may hope against bad fate but one accepts it as the other and absolutely natural side of fortune's coin. Love is the same. Little Augie takes it, savors it, tosses it away, with some regret, perhaps—the way one might have a favorite drink. Certain rituals must be performed, of course, not the least of all a love beating, for "a beating was an act of singular intimacy between a gal and her man" (94).

Bontemps achieves remarkable unity between language, plot (what little there is of it), and characterization. His descriptive and narrative prose is equally effective even though there is greater abundance of description. When Little Augie is at the height of his first success, he decides that he must dress in a mode that befits his new station in life:

> His high-roller had tiny naked women worked in eyelets in the crown. His shirts had two-inch candy-stripes of purple, pink, green, or orange, and the sleeves hung so low they covered his knuckles. The cuffs were fastened with links made of gold money, and just below them on Augie's third finger a rich diamond flashed opulently. His watch charm was a twenty-dollar gold piece, and his shoes had mirrors in the toes and dove-colored uppers with large pearl buttons. (25)

Another strong feature of the novel is the natural rendering of the language spoken by his characters. It is a rich and colorful idiom, unique in its black mode and full of incomparable humor. Here, for instance, is Augie scorning black women: "Black womens is onlucky. . . . they is evil, too, lak black cats. I wouldn't spit on one was she on fire" (26). Later, he declares his interest in a "high yellow" in language that can be thought of as pure Augie: "Yella gal, I loves you lak a hoss loves cawn, lak a fly do 'lasses. I loves you worser'n a hog loves to waller" (43). This elemental candor transcends the crudity one might attach to such similes. This is true throughout the novel, for Little Augie's mode of expressing himself is consistent with his character and his setting. The tone of the novel is aided, indeed sustained, through the author's effective use of language and diction.

This novel, coming on the heels of the Harlem Renaissance, succeeded better than many of the other novels by black writers because Bontemps concentrated on the chronicle of his hero and used racial and folkloric material only when it advanced his story. The mores of the South, the habits of common Negroes, and the racing world near the turn of the century are given an important yet balanced treatment in the novel. This fusion of the important and lesser segments of one type of black life, the treatment almost in toto of this microcosmic black world, relates directly to the Renaissance concerns of recreating the black past and of creating believable black fictional characters.

The novel form allows the writer freedom to develop characters, theme, and situation expansively. Therefore, it is not surprising that the Harlem Renaissance writers produced a large number of novels. These books provide sociological, cultural, and educational insights into the lives of a segment of the American populace who were denied basic rights and privileges. Neither is it surprising that the writers were strongly inclined to fiction in the realistic mode, chiefly because of the need to engage directly with "life" as it is lived by blacks from all social strata.

It is perhaps simplistic, then, to reiterate the entanglement and preoccupation the Negro writer of the 1920s had with his color and his role in American society. The writer's color, indeed, colored his themes: the Negro novelist by his act of being became his own metaphor. To expand this metaphor, he wrote novels that emphasized several themes:

1. Black struggle for self-assertion (e.g., *The Walls of Jericho, Not Without Laughter)*
2. Prejudice (e.g., *The Blacker the Berry, There Is Confusion*)
3. Passing (e.g., *Passing, Plum Bun*)
4. White violence (e.g., *Fire in the Flint, Dark Princess*)
5. "Tragic mulatto" (e.g., *Quicksand, Cane*)
6. Black vitality, humaneness, etc. (e.g., *Home to Harlem, One Way to Heaven*)

This brief overview of selected novels by Harlem Renaissance writers poses some questions, however, that seem inevitable for those of us who seek a fuller understanding of the movement as a whole. There is, for instance, a nebulous picture of the sort of artist these writers wanted to be. McKay and Thurman discuss this in their novels, to be sure, but when one is faced with the whole body of fiction from this period, there remains a suspicion that this was a fiction of naïveté. There is an artlessness in a novel that reflects belief in the platitudes of his times. Certainly many of the black novelists encumbered their books with ideas, people, and situations that did not get transformed into good fictive art. As Ralph Ellison has said, "People who want to write sociology should not write a novel."

A novelist is, after all, a person involved in an imaginative art. One could also argue about the moral obligation of the artist, but this might obscure another problem related to the one mentioned in the preceding paragraph. Although it may not be apparent from the abbreviated discussion of the previously mentioned novels, black writers exhibited a measure of faith in America that is amazing. The war injected an air of futility and disillusionment into the spirit of white writers. Black writers, on the other hand, saw the war as a wedge into the block of isolation that blacks had been facing in American society. Blacks were preening themselves to jump into a world formerly denied to them; whites were fleeing this world because, as Pound put it in the poem, "E. P. Ode Pour L'Election de Son Sepulchre" (from *Hugh Selwyn Mauberley*), the world was "an old bitch gone in the teeth./ . . . a botched civilization."

One can argue about the role and responsibility of the artist, about why so many of the novels of this period failed despite the fact that portrayal of black life by black writers was truer than that by white writers. But one overall weakness that is hard to assess is the matter of the technical flaws rampant in so many of the novels. The headiness of being so quickly "discovered" may have had something to do with the careless performance of some of these novelists. Perhaps the conflict between producing art and propaganda (or, art or propaganda) was the culprit. Nick Aaron Ford certainly thought so, for he wrote: "Since the Negro novelist has not produced even a first rate novel, is he not justified in laying aside the pretentions of pure artistry and boldly taking up the cudgel of propaganda? . . . I am inclined to think so."[22] Some of the publishers and editors must also share the blame.

The contemporary reader, however, must realize one other important observation: the black artist of this period, despite the popular assumption (based quite often on reading Hughes's essay), was an intellectual rather than a stylistic rebel. Aside from Toomer, McKay, and Hughes, the black writer hardly experimented with form and seemed, in essence, to forswear deeper involvement with the "inner processes" (Erich Auerbach's expression in *Mimesis* that describes the writer moving into the mind of his characters). Instead, the argument of these writers was with interpretations of the black man's various modes of living and his place in American society. Therefore, experimentation with time sequences, syntax, and delineation of characters, for instance, was a minor (if real) feature of the Harlem Renaissance writers.

The novelistic contributions of this group of writers cannot be dismissed cavalierly, either, in Johnsonian terms (i.e., it is remarkable that they wrote at all), because the publication of these novels, in the final analysis, had a few positive results:

1. Black life was more accurately portrayed.
2. Black writers were proving that they were a real force in American life.
3. The novels served as a warning to white writers that they could no longer trifle with the black character.
4. The novels proved that there was a wealth of material concerning Negroes yet to be explored.
5. A black aesthetic was gradually being formulated.
6. These writings formed a new and stronger bridge to the past for black writers who would come after the Harlem Renaissance writers.

This shifting of mimetic art from white to black interpreters helped to strengthen black selfhood, and this trend laid the literary foundation for black writers who would carry forward the search for blackness through less conventional, more militant artistic modes of expression.

NOTES

1. Dorothy West, "Elephant's Dance," *Black World* 20 (November 1970): 85.

2. Theophilus Lewis, "Wallace Thurman Is Model Harlemite," *New York Amsterdam News,* n.d. (Thurman File: Beinecke Library, Yale University).

3. Langston Hughes, *The Big Sea* (New York: Hill and Wang, 1963, c. 1940), p. 235.

4. Walter White, *Fire in the Flint* (New York: Knopf, 1924), p. 47.

5. Walter White, *Flight* (New York: Knopf, 1926), p. 295.

6. Claude McKay, *A Long Way from Home* (New York: Lee Furman, 1937), p. 112.

7. William Stanley Braithwaite, "The Novels of Jessie Fauset," *Opportunity* 12 (January 1934): 26.

8. Jessie Fauset, *There Is Confusion* (New York: Boni, 1924), pp. 284-285.

9. Jessie Fauset, *Chinaberry Tree* (New York: Negro University Press, c. 1931, 1969), p. ix.

10. Florence Smith Vincent, "There are 20,000 Persons 'Passing' Says Noted Author," *The Pittsburgh Courier,* 11 May 1929.

11. George S. Schuyler, "The Negro-Art Hokum," *The Nation* 122 (16 June 1929): 662.

12. Ibid.

13. Ibid.

14. Ibid.

15. Ibid., p. 663.

16. George S. Schuyler, *Black No More* (New York: Macmillan, 1971). All subsequent quotes will have page numbers included in the text in parentheses.

17. Northrop Frye, *Anatomy of Criticism* (Princeton: Princeton University Press, 1957), p. 224.

18. *New York Herald Tribune Books,* 1 February 1931, p. 5.

19. Robert A. Bone, *The Negro Novel in America* (New Haven: Yale University Press, 1965), p. 120.

20. Arna Bontemps, *God Sends Sunday* (New York: Harcourt, 1931), p. 3. All subsequent quotes will have page numbers included in the text in parentheses.

21. Belief in special powers for those born with a caul (i.e., the membrane enclosing a foetus which sometimes envelops the face at birth) is a significant belief among Africans and Jamaicans. "A child born with a caul is believed to be strong in combatting all evil spirits" (p. 197, Writers Program, Georgia, *Drums and Shadows* [Athens: University of Georgia Press, 1940]).

22. Nick Aaron Ford, *The Contemporary Negro Novel: A Study in Race Relations* (Boston: Mesdor Publishing Co., 1936), p. 102.

seven

THE SHORT STORY

With few exceptions (e.g., Toomer, Fisher), the black writer of the 1920s gravitated to poetry or the novel, or both. Relatively few were attracted to the short story genre. Many of the short stories that did appear were limited in scope and form, numerous examples of which were published in Negro-owned periodicals. While the output of the individual short story writers was meagre, the total number of stories that appeared in magazines (primarily *The Crisis* and *Opportunity*) is surprisingly large.

Zora Neale Hurston, who was to grow artistically after the 1920s, was one of the better Harlem Renaissance writers of short fiction. She exhibited a strong feeling for the form, a leaning which may have been a major factor in her subsequent interest in the Negro folk tale. One writer who showed strong early promise, John F. Matheus, devoted more and more time to teaching, reviewing, and translating after the late 1930s. Dorothy West also displayed a talent for short story writing.

Although she was rather on the coattails of the Harlem Renaissance movement, she incorporated into her fiction the Renaissance concerns for presenting the black man in a humane, realistic, and multidimensional manner. Rudolph Fisher, however, was the most polished practitioner of the art.

In addition to Hurston, Matheus, West, and Fisher, there were the talented Claude McKay, Arthur Huff Fauset, and Cecil Blue. The stories of Langston Hughes, for the most part, were to come later. Eric Waldrond's best stories were uniquely West Indian; hence, they should be examined as Caribbean literature. (Some of his stories, which appeared in *Opportunity*, seem to be sketches or miscellaneous commentary rather than bona fide short stories.)

In *The New Negro*, Alain Locke declared that "the artistic problem of the Young Negro has not been so much that of acquiring the outer mastery of form and technique as that of achieving an inner mastery of mood and spirit."[1] Too many examples prove him wrong, however. The short story more than any other literary genre demonstrates the technical weaknesses of many of the young Harlem Renaissance writers. Another problem was the limited audience for fiction dealing chiefly with the Negro experience. As the compilers of *The Negro Caravan* pointed out:

> The short story as a literary form in America has always been intended primarily for popular magazine publication; . . . In this medium, more than in others, the Negro author faces the dilemma of the divided audience. With the exception of the journals [*The Crisis* and *Opportunity*] of two Negro organizations . . . and a few fugitive publications, there have been no magazines with a primarily Negro audience in which writers could place their short stories. . . . The necessity for magazine publication has affected the Negro short story profoundly.[2]

And, yet, these young writers did produce some good short stories. The form was perfect for the purpose of brief illumination of selected segments of Negro life or for sharp portrayals of intense emotional moments. The need for this form of artistic expression, then, was an important feature of Harlem Renaissance writing that has been neglected by most literary reviewers of this period. Some of these writers surely deserve attention.

Rudolph Fisher, the master Harlem Renaissance craftsman of the short story, produced some of the more memorable literature in that period. He was a full-time physician (a radiologist), a book reviewer, essayist, and novelist, but his reputation today is based primarily on his skill in depicting Negro life in the short story. He died at the age of thirty-seven in 1934, during the same week that Wallace Thurman died. Fisher's and Thurman's lives drew to an end like a symbolic coda to the Harlem Renaissance itself: each represented the extremes of the period: Thurman, the bohemian, and Fisher, the bourgeois. Fisher, in particular, represented the solidly talented writer who could have given substance in depth to the movement. The period of "Negromania" was over, and a more urgent sociological literature—not quite in the balanced, sane mode employed by Fisher— was demanded. His legacy to the future, however, was not negligible.

When Henry James enjoined other writers to "Dramatize! Dramatize!" Rudolph Fisher must have heard the master's voice. Fisher orders the experience of Negro life in sensitive dramatizations. Nowhere is this better accomplished than in two of his best stories, "The City of Refuge" and "Miss Cynthie." Both stories illustrate Fisher's ability to transform life into art through control of characterization, plot, and diction, and insistence on a single effect at the story's conclusion.

The dual theme in "The City of Refuge" is the death of innocence and the black man's ability to transcend disillusionment. The story centers on King Solomon Gillis, a large, innocent, ignorant black who "had shot a white man and, with the aid of prayer and an automobile, probably escaped a lynching."[3]

Fisher places the protagonist immediately into the setting, that home of homes for the Negro, Harlem, which Fisher ironically defines as a "city of refuge." The author knows this is not always true, and his story is illustrative of the fact that Harlem, like the South, can be a place of confinement. Graphically, the story is constructed in the following manner:

I	II	III
Introduction: setting & characters (Harlem, Gillis, Uggam)	*Plan for entrapment* is set up	*Further development of entrapment scheme*
Definition-Theme: outward aspect of Harlem as a "city of refuge"	Subnote: Gillis lives in a confining room, one "half the size of his hencoop back home."	Contrast between innocence (Gillis) and evil (Uggam)

IV	V	VI
Setup, which will lead to *entrapment*, effected.	*Discovery of setup by police. Entrapment scheme by police & Gabrielli to catch Gillis* (who is always being manipulated, set up)	*Capture* (i.e., *enslavement*) of Gillis.
Story will have a downward movement from this point.		Subnote: Gillis is trapped in a cell-like underground cabaret, a hell.

The story is one of continual movement towards the entrapment and downfall of King Solomon Gillis. There is an added touch of irony in the name of the protagonist; the Biblical king has come down through literary history as the archetypal wise man, but King Solomon Gillis is far from wise. The story, indeed, relates with vivid economy just how unwise King Solomon Gillis is. Through flattery and guile and an eye for exploitation, Mouse Uggam, a resourceful drug pusher from Gillis's home town, uses him to pass along drugs without his understanding what he is doing. The set-up to trap King Solomon is planned in the second section where the subsidiary theme of confinement is stressed as well.

In the third section of the story, Mouse Uggam tightens his hold on King Solomon. Mouse has an uncanny talent for seeing through people, and thus he gets a job for Gillis which, in turn, works within the plan to have King Solomon to pass along drugs unsuspectingly. This section is rich in its evocation of Harlem language, atmosphere, and characterization. The American Negro's contempt for his black brothers from the West Indies is also deftly portrayed through attitude and dialect. Fisher's superior talent for realistic dialogue is in evidence in this section. In section four, Mouse Uggam sets up King Solomon's participation in drug pushing, and in the following section Tony Gabrielli, the owner of the store where Gillis works, sets Gillis up for entrapment by the police. The city of refuge is about to lose its character of sanctuary for one who symbolically and figuratively has fled another country. The last scene is laid, significantly, in a cavernous cabaret: it provides a contrast to King Solomon's first view of Harlem when, coming up from the subway, he was like "Jonah emerging from the whale" (21). Now he is in a place of entertainment that is in a low basement, reached by descending a "narrow, twisted staircase" (33). This is King Solomon Gillis's hell, although, as he is arrested (and deserted by Mouse Uggam who is, figuratively, a rat), he exudes an air that "had something exultant about it" (36). He is still a true believer in the black city with its "cullud policemans," and despite his end he retains his humanity and a deep satisfaction in his racial identity.

Fisher was a traditionalist in his approach to literature. Hence, it is not surprising that "The City of Refuge" has the traditional short story form: a recognizable beginning, middle, and end. The story also exhibits Fisher's genuine ability to penetrate the black character with complete understanding.

His effortless, extraordinarily skillful delineation of character is revealed in one of his last stories, and perhaps his best, "Miss Cynthie."

Harmony between the ages is played out beautifully in this
story. A stanza from Wordsworth fully expresses the theme
and movement of "Miss Cynthie":

Dust as we are, the immortal spirit grows
Like harmony in music; there is a dark
Inscrutable workmanship that reconciles
Discordant elements, makes them cling together
In one society.[4]

As one critic has written, "Reconciliation between the genera-
tions is the theme of this story."[5] The theme is worked out
almost melodiously, a talent that does not surprise those who
knew "Bud" Fisher. He was a fine musician who had spent
some time arranging Negro spirituals. He was a singer also and,
according to Langston Hughes, sang with Paul Robeson when
Fisher and Robeson both were in college.[6]

Miss Cynthie, drawn with love and humor, represents the
black grandmother archetype: shrewd, skeptical, religious,
loving, giving, forgiving, and wise. As she says of New York
during her first moments of arrival (and on her first trip of
any kind), "Reckon places is pretty much alike after people
been in 'em awhile."[7] It will take a lot to impress Miss Cynthie.
She has come to visit her grandson, not knowing that he is a
dancer and singer in Harlem. She had wanted him to be a doctor
or preacher or at least an undertaker. For her, these professions
fit in with her ideals and her admonition to Dave, "Always mind
the house o' the Lord—whatever you do, do like a church-
steeple: aim high and go straight" (56). Dave's plan is to introduce her to his profession by taking her to the club where he
works, to let her see rather than to hear about what he does.
He takes a chance on knowing her well enough to prove what
he tells his wife, "She's for church and all, but she believes in
good times too, if they're right" (60). As the reader and Miss
Cynthie move from doubt to enlightenment and reconciliation,
Fisher's use of song and rhythm reinforces the theme of union
between the old and the young.

Fisher never loses sight of his desire to entertain as well as to reveal values held to be important to Negroes. Although Fisher was from the Negro bourgeoisie—his father was a minister—he was successful in depicting the black man from every strata of Negro society. This ability is reflected in the eight short stories which were published after "The City of Refuge," culminating in his portrayal of the various sorts of Harlemites in his novel, *The Walls of Jericho* (1928).

John Matheus was generally an optimist and a believer in the ultimate conciliatory nature of man. We sense this in all of his work, with the exception of "Clay," an impressionistic story pervaded by a mood of pessimism. In this story, as well as in "Fog," there is a notion that death is the equalizer, that death brings together divergent men into oneness. This prevailing motif in Matheus's work, the reconciliation between men, is seen most clearly in his long narrative, "Anthropoi."

Although "Anthropoi" suffers from too much narration and too little action, the characterizations of Bush Winter, "an oversized, swarthy, black-haired mulatto," and Demetrius Pappan, "an undersized, swarthy, black-haired Greek," are successfully two-dimensional.[8] Neither man is exceptional, but Pappan, despite his swarthiness, is able to take part in the Great American Dream of financial success because he is "white." At one period in his American life he is a shoe polisher, polishing even the shoes of Bush Winter, and later he is the prosperous owner of a soda parlor where Bush and his family are not allowed to sit and drink. Later, their sons fight in the "Great War"; each son's life is spared, and each son undergoes a change in self as a result of his war experiences. After the war, Bush Winter's son is no longer patient with second-class citizenship in a land made safe by his personal act of heroism (i.e., exposing himself to the constant possibility of being killed). Pappan's son, whose level of consciousness concerning people, right and wrong, and justice, has been raised, becomes indignant as he watches a Ku Klux Klan member rushing through town in a car with the American flag attached to it. This act of racist cowardice and ignorance arouses young Pappan to go see what will ensue. More Ku Klux Klan members enter town and there is a melee. The near-death of young Pappan during the ensuing riot brings his father to the realization that he and Bush Winter are "brothers under the skin": "They understood each other, these old, worn fathers, after all." The understanding blossoms, and in the end they are reconciled.

Matheus's social philosophy is dramatically displayed in his more important and famous story, "Fog." Although it is technically frail in style and transitional phrasing, its publication is nonetheless of great scholarly interest: it marks the modern beginning of the black writer's serious concern for writing a short tale that is both thematically and dramatically outside the folkloric tradition.

"Fog"[9] is more complex than the bare plot reveals: a group of persons, multiethnic and multiracial, are on an interurban tramcar that must cross a bridge to arrive at its destination. The bridge gives out, but the people on the vehicle have enough time to escape the car. The fright from being so near death draws these people together and obliterates their ingrained animosities toward one another. The theme of death, or near-death, as the "great equalizer," combined with the symbols of fog (density) and the bridge (a nexus for divergent sides), leads into the story's strong redemptive motif. The story might even be considered propagandistic in its espousal of the idea of the equality of all men.

The fog is the focal point in the tale: it is not only a physical presence to be acknowledged, it is also a personification of the mental and emotional fog that clouds understanding from man to man. At the end of the story, the author (unfortunately, rather awkwardly) spells out the fog's symbolism: "The fog still crept from under the bed of the river . . . but from about the hearts and minds of some rough, unlettered men another fog had begun to lift." In "Fog," Matheus achieves a unity of action and tone. He is successful in creating a total effect that is carefully conceived from a central idea, or, more specifically, a dominant incident. The descriptive language establishes the physical surrounding. The use of dialect functions on two distinct but substantive levels: to signify actual ethnic differences and to indicate how little these differences mean in a moment of human crisis, in a moment when the common bond of humanity must serve individuals in a manner that enables them to overcome immoral or weak customs of a specific society

The cast of characters is large and each is an obvious vehicle for the point that Matheus wishes to emphasize. Just as the fog operates on a level above a mere atmospheric element, each person is submerged as an individual in order to buttress the theme and resolution of the action. The two major weaknesses of the story are sometimes distracting, the use of clichés and the structural shakiness of shifting from one person to another within a short span of time. In the case of the latter weakness, it is inevitable that constant shifts in point of view in a short story will weaken the structure, for this is a technique better suited to the novel. As for clichés, there is no need, for instance, to use such phrases as "Madonna eyed Italian mother," "Court house, that citadel of Law and Order," or "The news spread like wildfire." The more serious flaws, however, are the constant shifting of action and the rotation of character presentations within a brief stretch of time. This accounts for Matheus's awkward transitional sentences, such as, "Now these series of conversations did not transpire in chronological order," and, later, the following superfluous statement: "What happened inside the heads of these men and women seemed to them to have consumed hours instead of seconds." Dorothy Richardson, Joyce, and Woolf were demonstrating brilliantly how a writer could avoid such awkward phrasing and yet be dramatically and emotionally effective. In any case, this was not a new issue for the fiction writer, inasmuch as Flaubert discussed it when he wrote about what he wanted to accomplish in one of his famous moments in *Madame Bovary*. Time and spatial sequences are demanding problems for the writer, but "Fog" would have been enhanced if Matheus had been able to discover more subtle forms of expression. After all—and this must be remembered when assessing Harlem Renaissance literature—Matheus and writers like him were working for the most part within traditional stylistic forms.

The story's action is a lateral movement from the particular to the universal: a metaphoric use of the tramcar for the universe, and a grouping together of diverse persons to represent a cross-section of mankind becoming one in a cataclysmic moment. The physical salvation of these people parallels the theme of spiritual redemption. This dangerous moment represents a brief period when inner terror converges with outward commotion to form a bridge of understanding between divergent characters. Redemption through revelation? The author seems to point toward this idea. Thus we see that each person is tested in this moment of near-death. Our attention is focused on types of reaction rather than on individual ones because we do not know any character intimately enough to care for him personally. As readers, we can come away from this story in much the same manner as Crane's correspondent in "The Open Boat": "they felt that they could then be interpreters." Each character in "Fog," although seen fleetingly, becomes an interpreter of the event that touches everyone.

The 1927 first-prize story in *Opportunity* by Cecil Blue, "The 'Flyer,' " seemed to mark the appearance of another talented writer.[10] But it was a talent unfulfilled, for his ultimate literary contribution was negligible.[11] This story, however, deserves some scrutiny as a part of the realistic literature of the Harlem Renaissance.

The plot of "The 'Flyer,' " so-called after a train in the story, is built up around a man's conflicting emotions when he is confronted by his own humanness and his own weakness. On a week-end trip to visit a sister, Tim Hawkins (a sharecropper or farm-hand—it is not clear which) meets and falls in love with a pretty young girl, "a certain cinnamon-colored girl, with large black eyes, round faced and full-bosomed." The two have their

tender, brief idyll. Tim, a married man, is perfectly aware of
the fleeting quality of the chaste affair (much kissing appears
to be the climax of this foray into infidelity). After returning
on the "Flyer" to his home town, Tim is perplexed to find his
house empty; it is clean, tidy, and unnaturally inhospitable.
Guilt about his acts and feelings drives him to assume that his
wife, Bessie, has left him. But her absence is discovered to be
due to an act of charity (Bessie had been helping the family of
a dead friend) and misunderstanding regarding the expected
time of Tim's return. Tim's release from fear and frustration
is immediate and unreflective, although he senses instinctively
that his life is set aright again, that he has disengaged himself
from the perils of the uncertain and the unknown. The "Flyer"
will pass by Tim Hawkins for many years, for a lifetime, perhaps, as a symbol of contrast—its freedom, Tim's confinement—
and Tim will always be aware of what it has meant in his life.

The central symbols expand into metaphor as the "Flyer"
is described as "black and powerful, with the power of twenty
sleek horses." This is Tim—a man who is strong and powerful.
And the train and Tim are one for a brief time in their pursuit
of freedom, the train to journey to and fro, Tim to journey
once to a distant town where he has a few days of freedom.
This is a blissful freedom when he has the opportunity to flirt
with a woman who is softness itself, the antithesis of his wife,
whom he describes as being "true steel." There is added conflict
within Tim because he is attracted to both types of woman
(his male ego, even when perplexed, must be served). The out-
come of the story is strongly foreshadowed in the following
passage: "Then the phenomenon [the "Flyer"] disappeared;
and with his eyes riveted on the glistening cliff behind which
the last coach had slipped out of sight, he felt for the smooth
handle of the pick."[12] Tim, the quasi-innocent country dweller
goes to the city on the "Flyer," but he will discover that he
must return to his home in quite the same manner as his hand
will reaffirm the presence of the pick handle. Indeed, Tim will
return to his daily labors.

Timothy Hawkins conforms to the type of male frequently found in the black literature of this period: the dreamer, the man who must work and live outside the circle of his aspirations, the misinterpreted man even among his own people or his loved ones. Dorothy West portrays such men, as does Jessie Fauset.

A primary structural weakness of "The 'Flyer' " is the narration of the heart of the story in flashback. The strengths—characterization, mood, and description— are weighty enough to counterbalance the deficiencies. It is especially artistically satisfactory as a short story when compared to other works that appeared in *Opportunity* the year before.

Zora Neale Hurston did not exhibit any self-consciousness toward the provincial characters she created and, consequently, there is a sinewy, folkloric quality to her short stories. Hurston's characters live, for the most part, in an all-black world; when the white impinges on the black, each race maintains his societal role with abiding conviction. Thus, Hurston's black characters do not suffer from the sort of alternative black self-hatred/prideful self-love/hate-envy of white and black that characterize many other Harlem Renaissance fictional creations (e.g., McKay's Ray, Toomer's Kabnis, Thurman's Mary Lou, or some of the characters of Dorothy West). Zora Hurston's fictional style and characterizations were both deeply influenced by the colloquial, folk atmosphere of her native Florida where she collected folklore materials in connection with anthropological work she was doing with Franz Boas.

Several of Hurston's stories were published in *Opportunity* and serve as a good introduction to her artistic leanings toward folk literature. Her first story was "Drenched in Light," which at once displayed her ability to avoid one of the glaring weaknesses of her fellow black short-story writers, characterization. This is not to say that this is the strongest feature of her writing,

but each person she created had a fullness of self while expressing a specific, unique culture. The naturalness of her narrative
style may derive from her interest in folklore. The quality of
her writing, unpretentious, somewhat colloquial, seems to grow
out of her facility with dialect and her understanding of the
psychology and motivation of country folk and the tales they
told her. Her strongest, perhaps most interesting and intense
story, "Sweat," certainly gives evidence of this facility. Even
some of her lesser tales are noteworthy: they help to reveal,
as Darwin Turner has said, that "she was one of the few
Southern-born Afro-American writers who have consistently
mined literary materials from Southern soil."[13]

In "Drenched in Light," Isis ("Isie") Watts is a vital, energetic
girl of eleven, full of liveliness, spunk, brimming joy, designated
by her neighbors as being "different."[14] Isis's intelligent vitality
sets her apart from others in her farmland community in Florida.
Clearly, Isis is Zora Neale Hurston as a young girl, or, at least,
Isis is as Zora remembered her childhood self. The force of
"Drenched in Light" lies in Hurston's portrayal of Isis in action
before the reader: Isis poised with a razor as she prepares to
shave her grandmother, Isis dancing ("she wheeled lightly about,
hand on hips, flower between her teeth"), Isis wading in the
water. The major weakness of the story derives from the author's
acquiescence to a need to accept white appreciation even if it
casts Isis into the role of the "happy darkie." The notion seems
uncharacteristic of Hurston's writing, although numerous persons who have written about her personality suggest that she
may have had a need for the paternalistic attitude of many of
the whites she encountered. The approval that the happy little
Isis derives from the white couple who pick her up is countered,
in part, by the parallel need of the white woman to have "a
little of her sunshine." The notion may have a distasteful, racial
aspect, but the author has succeeded in presenting a strong
character portrait and an interesting side-account of black life
in rural Florida.

In the story, "Spunk," Hurston places the action within an all-black setting.[15] The movement from beginning to end is effectively rendered in sequences calculated to enrich the folkloric strains of this tale. There is also a mythic quality to this story of a dead man's revenge on his wife's lover. Certainly it is more than just a tale that "reveals the fickleness of the mob."[16] The superstitiousness of the common black is portrayed, if somewhat superficially, and the unspoken philosophy of happy survival in a small, rural, all-black community underpins the simple plot of the tale. Spunk, whose character is developed from what others think and say of him (the reader encounters him only once), is a super-hero who meets his defeat through his first and only contact with fear. His true enemy is himself, not the bobcat which may be thought of as the reincarnation of the cuckold-husband. Although Spunk is acquitted of shooting Joe Kanty, Spunk's conscience does not free him of guilt. Thus, this he-man builds up a fear of the dead man that forces him to lose control of his actions. Spunk visualizes the dead Joe Kanty as the one who "pushes" him upon the electric tree-saw, and the other Negroes are not willing to disbelieve Spunk's fearful notion. Once laid low, the hero is no longer admired because there is no need to fear him. The one gesture of comfort given to him as he is dying (perhaps viewed as surety against Spunk's spirit) is to lay him "with his face to the East so's he could die easy." Now gone, Spunk becomes another part of the folklore of the past as the survivors continue with the business of living.

"John Redding Goes to Sea," one of Hurston's weakest stories because of its maudlin quality, is nonetheless successful in its portrayal of a strong relationship between an uneducated black farmer and his dreamy, wishful son.[17] As a boy, John Redding is considered different by his impatient mother and the villagers. It is noteworthy that, although John loves and respects his mother, it is with his father that he confides and explores the nature of his longing to wander. Here we have one of the few examples in black literature of a strong bond between father and

son presented in a positive manner. John's hope of going away
to sea is foreshadowed as doomed when some of the twigs John
fancies as boats get caught in weeds and cease their journey down
stream. John asks his father, "Do weeds tangle up folks, too,
pa?"[18] John also points out to his father (who claims to speak
sometimes "in parables") a pine tree that has the appearance of
"a skull wid a crown on,"[19] thereby drawing the reader closer
to the notion that John, worthy as he is, will never go to sea in
the manner he wishes. It is only in death, a heroic death, to add
a touch of irony, that John Redding makes his contact with the
sea; and it is only his father who, rejecting efforts to recover
the young man's body, understands the necessity for leaving
John in the river: "Leave him g'wan. He wants tuh go. Ah'm
happy 'cause dis mawnin' mah boy is goin' tuh sea, *he' goin'
tuh sea.*"[20]

The preponderant folk quality of the story is most strongly
felt in the opening section when his mother declares John has
a "spell on 'im." Then, preceding the revelation of John's
death, a screech-owl is heard and his mother shouts, in terror:
"dat's sho' sign uh death."[21] Doom is always forecast by the
mother, as if she would prefer to have John dead than to have
him drifting about in an effort to fulfill his dreams. Thus, the
mother is the realist, and the father, like the son, a dreamer.

Hurston successfully handled the important elements of
the short story form—plot, diction, narration, and, especially,
mood. Hence, we can overlook some of her more obvious
faults, such as stilted conversation when she is not using dialect, her intrusion in narrative passages, and the relating of
events as narration rather than as action. Hurston, however, does
succeed, where other writers often failed, in presenting stories
with a "preconceived effect" faithfully adhered to and achieved.

Arthur Huff Fauset wrote one remarkably good short story,
"Symphonesque," which was awarded the first prize in the
1926 *Opportunity* contest and later was included in the
O'Brien *Best Short Stories of the Year* collection.[22] "Sym-

phonesque" is a passionate, pulsing, tale of sexual desire, temptation, and resistance to both—a story of sin and salvation.

The author mingles black culture and myth in the orchestration of his tale. He makes effective use of musical terminology to indicate the emotional intensity of the story. Section I, *Allegro non troppo* and *Allegro vivace et capricioso*, introduces the reader to seventeen-year-old Cudjo, the principal character. Cudjo (note the strictly black name), awakening in his absolutely filthy cabin, proceeds to voice to himself a diatribe against the preoccupation of blacks with religion: "Al dis 'ligion ain't gittin' nobody nowheah. All it does, mek yo' feel good. Mek yo' feel lik yo' treading' on soft cusions in Gawd's he'b'n." Just before these thoughts, Cudjo had felt a "curious shiver [course] slowly through his body." What we have, then, is the author establishing a pattern which serves as a leitmotif—the sacred and the profane at war in Cudjo's body and soul. The pervasiveness of religion is also a prime feature of the story. Cudjo attempts to mock and dismiss religion, and refuses, symbolically, the aid of Heaven: "He looked into the heavens. . . . His eyes could not stand the glare." Cudjo the elemental man, a "noble savage," the archetypal primitive, walks on. Yet, in another world, in another setting, he might have been a god or a hero. As he walks on, Cudjo continues to rail against God and His black followers, for to submit to the will of a being one cannot see seems incomprehensible, indeed, perhaps undesirable, to Cudjo. Yet, at the end of Section I he is among the church members who are colorfully preparing for the riverside baptism ceremony. Is it possible that Cudjo will be baptized and saved on this day? The reader wonders whether this is a possibility as the next section unfolds.

Part II, *Crescendo/Religioso Furioso*, opens with a vivid portrait of the preacher who is preparing to baptize the unsaved: "He was a tremendous black figure with a large round stomach that almost bulged out of his blue vest. . . . his corpulent body seemed like a huge inflated balloon made of thick rubber swaying upon two large resilient pillars." There is a certain mockery in the author's description; it is difficult, however, to ascertain if this is intentional or accidental. Since the story is primarily told from Cudjo's point of view, we also wonder how he would express it if he had the talent to use words like the author.

A commanding figure in this section is the exhorter who intones brief, repetitive verses to intensify the religious fervor of the already excited group. Fauset echoes the rhythmic stress of the exhorter who urges the crowd to respond in a typically black religious call-and-response pattern. Thus, Fauset is able to demonstrate the black man's African cultural heritage with dramatic artistry.[23] The effect of this and other exhortations on Cudjo, along with the frenzied atmosphere, is electric and shamelessly emotional: laughing, screaming, and running amok briefly, Cudjo attempts to rescue a fainting young girl from baptismal immersion. Thrown out of the area of the baptism ceremony—symbolically excluded from the saved and those to be saved—Cudjo lies alone in a heap, isolated, confused (but not knowing why he is), while the baptism ceremony continues for people who have quickly forgotten that "black fool," that "outcast devil," Cudjo.

The third and final section is elaborately weighted down with the following musical notations: *Agitato/Agitato appassionato/Smorzando et tranquillo.* The agitation from the religious ceremony is transformed in Cudjo into sexual terms, for his body is now aflame with the sensual desires of the flesh. His object is Amber Lee, singing sensuously in tall bushes nearby, Amber Lee who "feels only herself, her budding self." Although she is a pure young girl in the story, there is a touch of Toomer's Karintha in Amber Lee. Both serve as the archetypal Eve, or whatever African counterpart exists, the fecund temptress, the essential female.

Despite his passionate desire to seize Amber Lee and possess her, Cudjo hides and hesitates: here is the friend of his childhood, his playmate of old, an undefiled companion of his present everyday life. When he does manage to seize her, the fear and reluctance he sees in her eyes cool his ardor. He frees her, in shame, from his inflamed grasp and manages to apologize:

     · Ah wouldn't hurt a hair on yo' head . . . Amber Amber
     Lee . . . un'stan' . . .? Jes' want to scare mah lil' Amber
     Lee.
     He placed her gently on the warm grass and did not even
     kiss her.[24]

His quelled passion is reminiscent of the wearied emotional
and physical condition of the young girl who fainted at the
baptism ceremony. She had been overwhelmed by the passion
of religion, he by the passion of lust. Who, indeed, will be saved?

Fauset has shaped his story in a fashion that shows a direct
outgrowth from the black oral tradition, both folk and religious.
The story is enhanced further by his skillful use of symbols
and symbolic language. The paralleling of Cudjo's sexual desires
with the emotionalism of the baptismal service is an extremely
effective narrative mode. Added to this is the masterful use
of the church as in part symbol, in part metaphor: the church
as the seat of the black man's emotional life, the church as the
real world of black folk. Cudjo's rejection of this segment of
his black self seems to boomerang and become a part of him
despite his expressed sentiments of reproval. Thus, he is unable
to carry out the inner urgings of his natural male inclinations
when face to face with Amber Lee.

It doesn't seem unnatural that Fauset adopted the folk style
for unfolding his tale; he was, after all, a collector of folk
material from Nova Scotia and the Mississippi Delta. The tone
of the story is established immediately: Cudjo, realizing that
there is "somepin' mattah wid mah soul,"[25] is assailed by
longings, fears, and personal revulsion. The intense heat of
the day reinforces the notion of the soul's oppressiveness. In
a way, the setting seems more African than Texan. The soul
will be purified in one's native land, symbolically if not actually.
Touches such as those describing the preacher's laugh as being
"like the midnight cry of a panicky jungle cat,"[26] or personifying Cudjo's feet ("Did they not have ten eyes, as many noses,
and mouths as well?")[27] further illustrate Fauset's preoccupa-

tion with the spiritual and folk ties of the Afro-American with the land of his primary origins.

One critic characterized the Harlem stories in Claude McKay's short story collection, *Gingertown*, as being "on a very low level" whereas the Jamaican tales were described as "more exotic and more plausible."[28] The Harlem stories, however, have a vigor deriving, perhaps, from the sordidness of their setting and their plots. In "High Ball," McKay displays excellent control of tone, characterization, and form.[29] The story moves meaningfully from beginning to middle to dénouement.

The ingredients for drama are inherent in the situation in which the reader finds the black protagonist, Nation Roe, a successful singer-composer-pianist. Roe, recently married to a white woman, is becoming aware of her dissatisfaction with their mode of living. She complains that his friends, especially his white friends, do not care for her company and, therefore, exclude her from their gatherings. Nation—a simple man, a man of truth and inbred integrity—disbelieves her accusations because his closest friends, "colleagues to whom real merit was a thing considered above color," have never changed their attitudes toward him since his (to them) unpalatable marriage. McKay's description of Myra, the white wife, is swift and revealing: "She was rather a bloated coarse-fleshed woman, with freckled hands, beet colored elbows, dull-blue eyes and lumpy hair of the color of varnish." As Nation's best friend, George Lieberman, tells him after they have a heart-to-heart discussion about Myra: " 'If we were talking about a fish Myra would want to gut it right on the table; if it was about pigs she'd bring in the slops from the pen.' " Myra, quite simply, was a slut.

Myra is the crucial focal point of the story because it is she who effects the enlightenment and change in Nation. Myra is the one who spends a good part of her life guzzling gingerale highballs and running about low-type cabarets with her lesbian friend, Dinah. Nation's instincts, which lead him to dislike

Dinah, are not alert to the same qualities in Myra. In the end, Nation must learn about his wife's rejection and betrayal of him after he has reached utter, yet unjustified, despair about the loyalty of his old friends. Insulting them, Nation flees to his home where he must bear the insult of insults, hearing his wife and her friends mocking him, calling him by a name Dinah had carelessly called him one day, "prune." Nation's final act of throwing out Myra and her friends leaves him alone with only the hurt of his knowledge. McKay has handled the story effectively enough to make this ending a natural and true conclusion.

Throughout the story the tone of gradual but impending devastating enlightenment about the character of Myra is maintained. Myra sets the pattern in motion by implanting the germs of doubt and distrust in Nation. The incidents that help to build towards the dénouement are significant in both tone and characterization. The tone, after all, influences both mood and character; if the tone is controlled, the purpose of a story is made clear and every movement and every character are governed by this control. McKay accomplishes this. For example, we see this when Nation is thrown into confusion in his effort to understand the mixed-up Myra:

'I would like to go to some of those down-town parties.'

'They're mostly stags, though. . . '

'Stags,' she sneered, '*you* men! Don't mind about me, Nation. In fact, I really don't want to go to those affairs. Honest I don't. It's just some sort of jealousy. I don't care about anybody, as long as Dinah sticks to me.'

'And me?' asked Nation. 'What about me?' He laughed.

'Oh you know! I don't mean you. I mean Dinah compared to those downtown snobs.'

'You're a strange mixture, Myra. I kaint tell just what you want. I wish I could, for I want to please you always.'

She drank another highball.

'Don't mind me, Nation. It's nothing really. I think I want things that I really don't want, but I have to want them because my friends think I should have them. I don't want anything and I want everything.'

'That's beyond me, Myra, like something outa big heavy books.' And he went to his room to dress.[30]

Moving closer to a despair he cannot fathom, Nation walks with his friend George down the streets after George has given his views about Myra (and after a subsequent unfortunate "racial" incident at George's home):

> A little later George and Nation left for the theatre. They strode along in silence. George desired to say something soothing to Nation, knowing that he was hurt, but he could not find a precisely appropriate phrase. Nation apprehended George's mood. He preferred that nothing further should be said about the incident, so he talked a great deal about nothing.
>
> At Broadway and Forty-third Street they parted a little awkwardly, each one going to his own theatre.[31]

There is in this scene a sense of the closeness between these two men, and there is also a sense of impending massive unhappiness awaiting both men. In the end, Nation's wrongheaded assessment of his friends and his diatribe against them wounds George in a manner that directly corresponds to Myra's damage to Nation's heart and ego.

The emotional effectiveness of the story derives from McKay's skillful handling of sequence and incident, characterization, and the full control he displays in narrative exposition and tone in the unfolding of this poignant tale.

In 1926 the second prize in the short story competition of the *Opportunity* contest was shared by Zora Neale Hurston for "Muttsy" and an unknown, first-published eighteen-year-old, Dorothy West, for her story entitled, "The Typewriter."[32] West said of herself at the time: "I was born in Boston . . . and educated in the public schools, for which, I must confess, I had

no great fondness. To be conventional, my favorite author is
Dostoevsky, my favorite pastime, the play. I am rather a reticent sort, but I am intensely interested in everything that goes
on about me."[33] This prize story was her first, she claims; it is
a strong beginning for an author who was to write a distinguished,
engrossing novel, *The Living Is Easy* (1948).

The unnamed protagonist of "The Typewriter" is a hard-
working, simple, honorable husband and father. He lives in
Boston, having moved there from the South in his young
manhood. He is a man now who admits to himself a disappointment with how his life has developed; his life is far below the
economic and social levels he had envisioned for himself when
he was a newcomer in Boston. "But, though he didn't know
it," the author writes, "he was not the progressive type. And
he became successively, in the years, bell boy, porter, waiter,
cook, and finally janitor in a down town office building." We
plunge immediately into the story that tells of this unachieving
man's daughter practicing, upon a rented typewriter, the writing
of business letters. To aid her, the father begins to dictate
imaginary letters to and from important business people (e.g.,
Rockefeller, J. P. Morgan). To round out the verisimilitude,
the father creates for himself the inflated persona whom he
calls Mr. J. Lucius Jones. What originates as a favor to help
his daughter achieve speed and accuracy with her stenography
and typing becomes a fantasy-world into which the father
hungrily escapes each evening, a fantasy-world where he trans-
forms himself into a superior, achieving man. The daughter—
the realist, an adultlike child in her materialist attitude— is
unaffected by her father's emotional and psychological approach
to their nightly exercise.

The daughter reaches a high level of proficiency, secures a
job, and returns the typewriter to the rental agency. When her
father discovers that the typewriter is gone his world is shattered:
"It burst upon him. Blinded him. . . Why this—this was the end!
The end of those great moments—the end of everything!" What
we have here is the portrait of a man of feeling who remains
unfulfilled in his psychological and emotional relationship with
his family. The influence of Dostoevsky here, and in a sub-

sequent story, "An Unimportant Man,"[34] is pervasive: the close identity of the father to his daughter evokes the Dostoevskian absorption with childhood and his belief in the incorruptible nature of children. It is only in the child's confrontation with the adult world that the process of ruination begins.

There is also the Dostoevskian tendency to emphasize confinement, in moral, psychological, emotional, and physical aspects: "He would never be able to get away from himself and the routine of year" ("The Typewriter"); and: "And in that instant Zeb wanted frantically to break into that line. He didn't want to go home to Minnie, and a fretful baby, and a mother whose reproachful eyes spoke her unsatisfied hopes" ("An Unimportant Man"). As it is, the men in both of these stories are confronted with incidents that thwart any escape from their confining world.

Dostoevsky's influence in these two stories (and in "Prologue to a Life") is implicit in the idea of salvation through suffering.[35] This notion, the downward path to redemption, can be charted in the following manner:

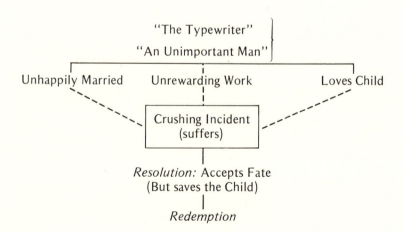

In "An Unimportant Man," the protagonist, Zeb, has finally passed his bar examination at the age of "barely forty." At the end of the story, he is faced with the necessity of retaking the exam because of a technicality unrelated to himself. But Zeb, who has failed the examination on his first two tries, knows he cannot repeat the successful performance of his third try. He faces the realization that he will not escape the dreary destiny of other "unimportant" men. Zeb then turns his attention from himself to his daughter who is being repressed by her mother and grandmother. He decides to try persuading her to use her fine brain to succeed in some unnamed, professional career in place of seeking a dancer's way of life: "He must save Essie from the terrible fate that had all but crushed his spirit." She must not become trapped as he had. This freedom and independence, gained through education, he thought, would prove more satisfactory to her in the end than a career based on her "childish whim," dancing in clubs and cabarets.

In "The Typewriter" and "An Unimportant Man," West gives examples of men caught up in the inescapable maze of an adulthood inferior to the one they had anticipated. Both men are childlike, and they satisfy themselves through the lives of their children, even though their communication with the children is partially defective. In "The Typewriter," the other side of the father's nature, the submerged, uncharted area of his emotional life, is suddenly fulfilled by the fantasy-world he creates for his daughter's mechanical practice upon the typewriter. And Zeb, in his determination to help his daughter, enlarges his inner life as well. Through "J. Lucius Jones," Zeb has performed an act that will save his daughter from the unfulfilled life he has.

The men in West's stories are unachieving, disappointed persons who still have retained a measure of innocence. This artlessness sets them apart spiritually from the women in her stories who, discontented and frustrated by the confinement of their place in life, succumb to the realities of their second-rate lives. They retreat into an overtly bitter, unredemptive

existence: Hanna Byde (in the story of the same name[36])
laughs spitefully about botching up a suicide attempt and is
contemptuous of the baby she is carrying; Net (the wife in
"The Typewriter") constantly berates her husband; and Lily
("Prologue to a Life"), happy only as a mother, spurns a meaningful relationship with her adoring husband. The women are
neurotics; the men are psychologically emasculated by women
and society. Even the financially successful husband in "Prologue
to a Life" is a victim of the emotional states of his wife and
mother.

West's psychological soundness in her stories is not always
supported by an adequate fictional style. She has many poorly
constructed sentences, awkward descriptive clauses, overuse
of the past tense, a tendency to intrude as author, clichés, and
self-conscious dialogue that is often completely lifeless. Here
are two examples:

"Prologue to a Life," pp. 7-8:
It was on the last day of March, going all too meekly like
a lamb [the reader has no idea why this is so], that Lily,
in her kitchen, making raisin-stuffed bread pudding the
twins adored, sat down suddenly with her hand to her
throat, and her heart in a lump against it.

"An Unimportant Man," pp. 21, 23, 27:
Little waves of joy rolled over him.

He entered the bathroom then, his cheeks burning with
resolute purpose.

He beamed his gratitude.

West, in transcending her faults, managed to portray a special
milieu of black life that other black short story writers rarely
touched upon—the frustrated, urban middle class in its struggle
to grasp the goods of American life. West attempted to explore
the duality of human nature through these people, and in
doing so she contributed some interesting, creditable stories
that literary historians should not overlook.

Ever since Poe, Americans have considered the short story their special literary territory. It has been a form, however, practiced by few when compared numerically with novels and poetry. Still, American writers have been the foremost practitioners of this art form, a form which some will argue Hemingway brought to its apogee. The short story, for all of its brevity, is a difficult medium in which to excel, and the critical standards of the editors who publish stories are high and rigorous. When the young Negro writer was being discovered during the 1920s, he had a tendency to overproduce; but, for some reason, he did not appear to know what to do with the short story form. As a result, the stories that were published are frequently technically uneven. Part of the problem may stem from what the editors of *The Negro Caravan* observed: "Few short stories by Negro writers exist for the sake of the story alone."[37] The carryover from the slave narrative tradition may have had a hampering effect. That is, the psychological need to explain what it was to be a Negro in a racist society, the desire to portray what injustice does to sensitive, rejected human beings, the sense of responsibility "to the race," all must have influenced plot, characterization, and mode of exposition. Most of the mediocre writers were defeated by stylistic deficiencies. As it was put in *The Negro Caravan*: "In few of these stories is there humor or deft characterization or psychological understanding; these elements are sacrificed to the burning message."[38]

A perusal of *The Crisis* and *Opportunity* and, in lesser part, *The Messenger,* offers a fascinating glimpse of the earnest struggle to conquer the short story form. Writers such as those mentioned earlier, in addition to John Young, Louis L. Redding, Eugene Gordon, Jessie Fauset, and Marita Bonner all tried their hands at the genre, though with limited and variable artistry. If their stories fell short of great art, it is easy enough to suggest that many of their readers were not concerned with this matter anyway. Generally, the black writer was not yet prepared to give serious artistic regard to a form that required presenting the essence of a life, or lives, in fragments of time and space.

That organic design leading towards a "unique or single effect," that very compact type of fiction, the short story, was never to reign during the Harlem Renaissance. But it was the country cousin of the Renaissance, and even country cousins must be acknowledged.

NOTES

1. Alain Locke, *The New Negro* (New York: Boni, c. 1925, 1927), p. 48.

2. *The Negro Caravan* (New York: Dryden Press, 1941), p. 10.

3. Rudolph Fisher, "The City of Refuge." In John Henrik Clark, ed., *American Negro Short Stories* (New York: Hill & Wang, 1966), p. 22. All subsequent quotes will be taken from this edition, and page numbers will be included in the text in parentheses.

4. Wordsworth, "The Prelude," Bk. 1, 1. 340.

5. Oliver Louis Henry, "Rudolph Fisher: An Evaluation," *The Crisis* 78 (July 1971): 153.

6. Langston Hughes, *The Big Sea* (New York: Hill & Wang, c. 1940, 1963), p. 241.

7. Rudolph Fisher, "Miss Cynthie." In *The Negro Caravan*, p. 55. All subsequent quotes will be from this edition, and page numbers will be included in the text in parentheses.

8. John F. Matheus, "Anthropoi," *Opportunity* 6 (August 1928): 229-232. (Note: story title is misspelled on p. 229).

9. John F. Matheus, "Fog," *Opportunity* 3 (May 1925): 144-147.

10. Cecil Blue, " 'The Flyer,' " *Opportunity* 6 (July 1928): 202-206, 216.

11. Blue was a professor at Lincoln University (Missouri) until his retirement in 1973.

12. Blue, " 'The Flyer,' " p. 203.

13. Darwin T. Turner, *In a Minor Chord; Three Afro-American Writers and Their Search for Identity* (Carbondale: Southern Illinois University Press, 1971), p. 98.

14. Zora Neale Hurston, "Drenched in Light," *Opportunity* 2 (December 1924): 371-374.

15. Zora Neale Hurston, "Spunk," *Opportunity* 3 (May 1925): 171-173.

16. Turner, *In a Minor Chord*, p. 99.

17. Zora Neale Hurston, "John Redding Goes to Sea," *Opportunity* 4 (January 1926): 16-21.

18. Ibid., p. 16.

19. Ibid.

20. Ibid., p. 21.

21. Ibid., p. 16.

22. Arthur Huff Fauset, "Symphonesque," *Opportunity* 4 (June 1926): 178-180, 198-200.

23. Henry H. Mitchell, *Black Preaching* (New York: J. B. Lippincott, 1970), p. 95.

24. Arthur Huff Fauset, "Symphonesque," p. 200.

25. Ibid., p. 178.

26. Ibid., p. 198.

27. Ibid., p. 178.

28. Stephen H. Bronz, *Roots of the Negro Racial Consciousness* (New York: Libra, 1964), p. 87.

29. Claude McKay, "High Ball," *Opportunity* 5 (May 1927): 141-144 and (June 1927): 169-172.

30. Ibid., p. 143.

31. Ibid., p. 170.

32. Dorothy West, "The Typewriter," *Opportunity* 4 (July 1926): 220-222, 233-234.

33. "Our Authors and What They Say Themselves." *Opportunity* 4 (July 1926): 189.

34. Dorothy West, "An Unimportant Man," *The Saturday Evening Quill* (Boston) (June 1928): 21-32.

35. Dorothy West, "Prologue to a Life," *The Saturday Evening Quill* (Boston) (April 1929): 5-10.

36. Dorothy West, "Hannah Byde," *The Messenger* 8, no. 7 (July 1926): 197-199.

37. *Negro Caravan*, p. 12.

38. Ibid., p. 13.

eight

THE MINOR POETS

The task of giving definition and shape to the dominant features of Negro poetry during the 1920s can be understood best by leafing through the pages of *Opportunity* or *The Crisis*. For example, on page 23 of the January 1926 issue of *Opportunity*, there are two poems that illustrate the difficulty of trying to categorize essential elements of Harlem Renaissance poetry. Here we read "To Midnight Nan at Leroy's" by Langston Hughes, with its rhythmic opening lines—

> Strut and wiggle
>   Shameless gal,
> Wouldn't no good fellow
>   Be your pal?

Below this graphic five-stanza verse is the rhyming, romantic quatrain by one of the youngest lyricists of this time: "Night," by Helene Johnson:

The moon flüng down the bower of her hair,
A sacred cloister while she knelt at prayer.
She crossed pale bosom, breathed a sad amen—
Then bound her hair about her head again.

The sheer bulk of Hughes's production of poetry, in addition
to his forceful expression of what he saw to be his role as a
writer, serves to explain his work. But there was a roster of
minor poets whose work appeared sporadically in the journals;
generally, the output of each was too scant to produce a book
of verse. Of those who did have a volume of poetry appear in
print (e.g., Georgia Douglas Johnson, Sterling A. Brown, James
Weldon Johnson), only Brown achieved a large measure of
success as a poet. There were other minor poets, however,
who unevenly display an interesting range of poems concerning
such subjects as love, death, the past, and the black world and
who published during the Harlem Renaissance years. Included
in this group are the following poets: Arna Bontemps, Waring
Cuney, Frank Horne, Anne Spencer, Gwendolyn Bennett, and
Helene Johnson.

Some poets, such as James Weldon Johnson, have given us
an exact explanation of the how and why of a poem. In his
autobiography, he relates how he came to write his major poetic
work, *God's Trombones:*

The research which I did in collecting the spirituals and
gathering the data for my introductory essay had an effect
on me similar to what I received from hearing the Negro
evangelist preach that Sunday night in Kansas City. This
work tempered me to just the right mood to go on with
the deepest revelation of the Negro's soul that has yet been
made, and I felt myself attuned to it. I made an outline of
the second poem that I wrote of this series. It was to be a
"funeral sermon." I decided to call it "Go Down Death."[1]

This sense of being "in touch with the deepest revelation of the
Negro's soul" is evoked immediately in the opening lines of
this poem:

Weep not, weep not,   [Oh-o-oh]
She is not dead;   [Yes, Lord!]
She's resting in the bosom of Jesus.   [Amen]
Heart-broken husband—weep no more;   [Amen]
Left-lonesome daughter—weep no more;   [Amen]
She's only just gone home.[2]   [A-men, A-a-men, O Lord!]

The litanylike, Negro call-and-response pattern is evident in this
verse: one can easily imagine the preacher calling the lines
Johnson has written and hear an aching response, such as that
above, from the bereaved family and the congregation. And
yet Johnson has accomplished this in the only terms acceptable
to him as poetic artist—in an idiomatic language euphonically
reminiscent of his people but eschewing the orthography of
Negro dialect. As he explained, he generated within himself
some of the emotional intensity apparent in the finished work:
"As I worked, my own spirit rose till it reached a degree almost
of ecstasy."[3] Finally, in the quest to find an appropriate title
for the completed work, Johnson decided upon the metaphor
of a trombone because "I had found it, the instrument and the
word, of just the tone and timbre to represent the old-time
Negro preacher's voice. Besides, there were the traditional jazz
connotations. So the title become *God's Trombones—Seven
Negro Sermons in Verse.*"[4]
    God's Trombones is drama to be heard and seen, just as the
medieval mystery plays functioned as entertainment and religio-
moral instruction. The verses cry out for recitation before an
audience in order to recreate what Johnson described as "the
fervor of the congregation, the amens and hallelujahs, the under-
tone of singing . . . the personality of the preacher . . . and, more
than all, his tones of voice."[5] There are places in the verse also
where one can envision a Eumenides-like chorus chanting:

And God rained down plagues on Egypt,
Plagues of frogs and lice and locusts,
Plagues of blood and boils and darkness,
And other plagues besides.
But ev'ry time God moved the plague
Old Pharaoh's heart was hardened,
And he would not,
No, he would not
Let God's people go.
And Moses was troubled in mind.[6]

Johnson achieves the tone and cadence of the folk preacher through a skillful blending of Biblical phrases, Negro spirituals, and his creative imaginings of the sermons which an articulate minister might chant to his congregation. One has to remember that there is (or was for a certainty in Johnson's time) a mystical interdependence between the black preacher and his congregation; this bond was in constant renewal through the words of the Lord that the parishioners received when listening to sermons. Of *God's Trombones*, Johnson says: "It was not my intention to paint the picturesque or comic aspects of the old-time Negro preacher—I considered them extraneous—my aim was to interpret what was in his mind, to express, if possible, the dream to which, despite limitations, he strove to give utterance."[7]

The reader of poetry, perhaps without articulating this idea, is moved emotionally by the writer's use of rhythm. Compare the long, soothing lines of the end of "Go Down Death" with the quick-paced, piercing lines from "The Crucifixion":

And Jesus took his own hand and wiped away her tears,
And he smoothed the furrows from her face,
And the angels sang a little song,
And Jesus rocked her in his arms,
And kept a-saying: Take your rest,
Take your rest, take your rest.[8]

. . . .

On Calvary, on Calvary,
They crucified my Jesus.
They nailed him to the cruel tree,
And the hammer!
The hammer!
The hammer!
Rang through Jerusalem's streets.[9]

The close patterning of the poem upon the Bible connotes a symbiotic relationship with Judaic history rather than a linkage with the black African heritage (excepting the preacher's diction, which Johnson thinks may have "some kinship with the innate grandiloquence of their old African tongues"[10]). The sentiment of a personal, active, unseen being (God) is pervasive, as is the notion of relief from suffering being achieved through death—the gateway, as it were, to heaven and, consequently, a release from earth's and man's imposed trials upon the ordinary person. This is Old Testament religion, reconstructed for the audience of a black church, and fashioned, once again, in such a vivid spiritual mode that it becomes drama itself intoned in a unique, poetic language.

Johnson created an ersatz dialect through euphony, skillful rhythmic patterns, and infrequent grammatical distortion. His successful synthesis of the linguistic style and contents of the Negro sermon and the Negro speech idiom (the felt sound, tone, structure) pointed the way toward a unique form of artistic expression.

Sterling Brown did not agree with Johnson's position on dialect; many of Brown's poems indicate this clearly by his strong use of the common black's dialect. But Brown is a questionable person to be thought of as a *participant* in the Harlem Renaissance because, despite his winning first prize in poetry (Holstein Poetry Section) in the 1927 *Opportunity* contest, his major work started to appear in the 1930s. And, approxi-

mately thirty years after the height of the Harlem Renaissance,
Brown had this to say about the period: "The New Negro is
not to me a group of writers centered in Harlem during the
second half of the twenties. Most of the writers were not Harlemites; much of the best writing was not about Harlem, which
was . . . no more Negro America than New York is America."[11]

That first prize poem, "When de Saints Go Ma'chin' Home,"
indicates the direction in which Brown was heading:

> *Oh when de saints go ma'chin' home.*
> "Ole Elder Peter Johnson
> Wid his corncob jes a puffin'
> And de smoke a rollin'
> Like stormclouds out behin'
> Crossin' de cloud mountains
> Widout slowin' up fo' nuffin'
> Steamin' up de grade
> Lak Wes' bound No. 9."
>
> . . . .
>
> *"Whuffolks,"* he dreams, *"will have to stay outside*
> *Being so onery."* But what is he to do
> With that red brakeman who once let him ride
> An empty going home? Or with that kindfaced man
> Who paid his songs with board and drink and bed?
> Or with the Yankee Cap'n who left a leg
> At Vicksburg? *Mought be a place, he said,*
> *Mought be another mansion fo' white saints*
> *A smaller one than his'n . . . not so gran'.*
> *As fo' the rest . . . oh, let them howl and beg."*[12]

Thus, he captures the racy idiom of ordinary black folk, the
country people who work hard and drink hard and speak wisdom with raw, undiluted frankness. Within the speech pattern
we also catch a flavor of the philosophy and psychology of
those black folk: life has been hard and unfair, yes, but even
among the "whuffolks" there are some who may be redeemed

in the end. It is clearly a black and white world, with each side facing the other in social and moral combat. This is why Brown was unhindered by the pretentions of other black poets and was able to reach back into the black past. He is not caught up in that dichotomized world of "two-ness" DuBois described: for Brown, the black world has enough richness to sustain him. He has no white side warring with his blackness. His poetry obdurately attacks white racism, not in the plaintive fashions of Cullen and McKay, or the mocking manner of Hughes, but in a vigorous, accusatory manner, such as in "Old Lem" or "Strong Men." Brown's close identification with the earth derives from his numerous trips to the South in order to research folk material. What he found he made his own, without an intermediary to distill the experience for him. He captures the idiom of these people within the exact context of their quotidian existence. Alain Locke suggested this when he wrote:

> Sterling Brown has listened long and carefully to the folk in their intimate hours, when they were talking to themselves, not, so to speak, as in Dunbar, but actually as they do when the masks of protective mimicry fall. Not only has he dared to give quiet but bold expression to this private thought and speech, but he has dared to give the Negro peasant credit for thinking.[13]

Brown's poetry, then, grows from his emotional and spiritual attachment to the agrarian Negro, the true black person, according to the poet. It is the agrarian Negro, Brown tells us, who has kept alive the traditional ambiance of black literature. What Brown appears to be doing in his verse is to work in and around the soil and soul of his ancestors. In spirit, then, he was much like McKay—antiurban. But Brown's dislike of the city in his poetry was thorough, whereas McKay romanticized about its vitiating influence on the soul of the Negro.

In the recent translation of his book about Negro poets,
Jean Wagner states: "Brown was instinctively drawn to the
South, which he has traversed in every direction, listening to
the songs of his ethnic brothers on the very soil of their destiny,
ramote from the Harlem cabarets where others grew drunk on
gin."[14] Brown also agreed with James Weldon Johnson that the
black man was inextricably tied to the soil, but Brown's recrea-
tion of this actual and metaphorical bond was unromantically
and sometimes cruelly depicted. The soil was neither sustaining
nor comforting, it was often an enemy:

> Father Missouri takes his own.
> These are the fields he loaned them,
> Out of hearts' fullness; gratuitously;
> Here are the banks he built up for his children—
> Here are the fields; rich, fertile silt.
>
> . . . .
>
> Uncle Dan, seeing his garden lopped away,
> Seeing his manured earth topple slowly in the streams,
> Seeing his cows knee-deep in yellow water,
> His pig-sties flooded, his flower beds drowned
> Seeing his white leghorns swept down the stream—[15]

The same image can be found in several of his other poems,
such as "Children of the Mississippi," "Strange Legacies," and
"Riverbank Blues."

Southern Road, Brown's major book of poetry, was published
in 1932. It is divided into four sections, the last of which contains no dialect. In the "Introduction," James Weldon Johnson
concludes with the following judicious observation: "Mr. Brown
has included in this volume some excellent poems in literary
English and form. I feel, however, it is in his poems whose
sources are the folk life that he makes, beyond question, a distinctive contribution to American Poetry."[16] In shifting back
and forth between the rural and city scenes, Brown portrays a

memorable cast of characters, moods, and sentiments: "Maumee
Ruth," ruined by the city, "sniffing the 'snow,' " or unlucky,
gambling "Johnny Thomas," who "oughta had mo' sense/Dan
to evah git born." But there is pride, too, in "Strange Legacies":
"John Henry, with your steel driver's pride,/ You taught us that
a man could go down like a man." There is humor as well:

> Listen to the tale
> Of Ole Slim Greer,
>
> . . . .
>
> Nobody suspicioned
> Old Slim Greer's race
> But a Hill Billy, always
> Roun' the place.
>
> . . . .
>
> The cracker listened
> An' then he spat
> An' said, "No white man
> Could play like that. . ." [17] ("Slim Greer")

In the end, Slim Greer escapes. The depiction of his escape and
the silly panic of the whites is in the true vein of Negro humor.

Brown was also thoroughly conscious of the black man's
religious leanings and needs. In his poetry he approaches this
important segment of Negro life with both belief and cynicism.
Just as in "When de Saints Go Ma'chin' Home," there is sometimes present the humorous (or cynical?) illusion of the white
man finally getting his come-uppance when blacks go to heaven
(see "Sister Lou," for instance).

In Brown's poetry, there is the lingering notion that the
black man has control of his nature, even if the white man
and earth and sometimes God are unjust, cruel, or indifferent.
Because Brown is emotionally and psychologically rooted in
experiences of the native American black, his poetry exhibits
an overall belief in the black man's ultimate triumph over re-

straining obstacles which bar his way. An aura of realistic pessimism hangs over much of his work but it is relieved by humor, on one hand, and by faith in the future, on the other, as exemplified by his well-known inspirational poem, "Strong Men":

> One thing they cannot prohibit—
> > The strong men. . . coming on
> > The strong men gettin' stronger.
> > Strong men. . .
> > Stronger. . .[18]

Brown's poetry reflects the ambiance of a preindustrial world. His blacks are tied to the soil, inextricably bound in love, anger, and frustration. The poetic expression of this state of existence requires a language that is immediately visual and visceral. In this way, one notes a bond with one segment of Césaire's concept of négritude, the sense of alienation from the city and all that it symbolizes:

> Ma négritude n'est ni une tour ni une cathédrale
> elle plonge dans la chair rouge du sol.[19]

Simultaneously, the reader senses an underlying sentiment (conscious or unconscious—who can say?) against the Western (i.e., Euro-Anglo-American) system of aesthetics because of the direct, unadorned language and the absence of multiple levels of meaning. To paraphrase a contemporary black comic, Flip Wilson, Sterling Brown seems to be saying that what we read is what we get. Therefore, we hear and see the symbolic transformation of the African heritage (rhythm, tone, mood, subject-matter) into the linguistic idiom of the common black Southerner.

It is interesting to reflect again that both Brown and James Weldon Johnson pointed the way toward the tone and, partially, the style of poetry being produced by young black poets today. This observation heightens their historical importance but does

not alter their roles as minor poets during the Harlem Renaissance period.

When we speak of a "Renaissance man," we think of someone with a wide range of interests and talents, a person of taste,
culture, learning, and intelligence. The black Renaissance man
during the Harlem Renaissance period was James Weldon
Johnson; in our time, until his death in June 1973, the Renaissance man was Arna W. Bontemps. Poet, storyteller, essayist,
lecturer, teacher, librarian, and social historian, Bontemps more
than any other person brought the Harlem Renaissance era
alive for us because of his intellectual and emotional commitment
to this decade. At that time he was primarily a poet; his output, although small, is poetry of memorable beauty. His sure hand at poetic techniques, combined with an unmuddled sense of thematic
direction, demonstrate his genuine talent for verse writing.

The editors of *The Negro Caravan* characterized Bontemps's
poetry as "generally mystical, philosophical, with an elegiac
quality." His prize-winning poem "The Return" (Pushkin Prize,
1927), justifies this evaluation. Moreover, this poem is a skillful
distillation of Bontemps's own deeply felt emotional experiences.
This passing back and forth of feeling and knowledge between
the poet and the reader places both in the domain of truth-
searchers. The emotion in "The Return" is sustained by the
imagery of the African homeland:

> Darkness brings the jungle to our room:
> The throb of rain is the throb of muffled drums.
> Darkness hangs our room with pendulums
> Of vine and in the gathering gloom
> Our walls recede into a denseness of
> Surrounding trees. This is a night of love
> Retained from those lost nights our fathers slept
> In huts; this is a night that must not die.
> Let us keep the dance of rain our fathers kept
> and tread our dreams beneath the jungle sky.[20]

The sensuality is beautifully heightened by the figurative
jungle setting:

> A moment we pause to quench our thirst
> Kneeling at the water's edge, the gleam
> Upon your face is plain: you have wanted this.
> Let us go back and search the tangled dream
> And as the muffled drum-beats throb and miss
> Remember again how early darkness comes
> To dreams and silence to the drums.[21]

The control of form and the almost elegant emotionalism are
reminiscent of Wallace Stevens's celebration of hedonism,
underpinned always by a poignant strain of romanticism.

Bontemps relies heavily on religious symbolism. The infusion
of Christian belief is obvious in such poems as "Golgotha Is a
Mountain," "Nocturne at Bethesda," and in many of his lesser
poems, such as "The Day-Breakers" and this fragment from
"God Give to Men":

> For black men, God,
> no need to bother more
> but only fill afresh his meed
> of laughter,
> his cup of tears.
>
> God suffer little men
> the taste of soul's desire.[22]

In a parallel manner, Bontemps relies on the emotional symbolism of the black man's past in his "racially" oriented poems.
These verses are rendered in an attenuated fashion that fosters
the belief that the black man's strong religious beliefs and
remembrance of an unfettered past make his plight bearable.

Bontemps fuses religious and racial elements in his most
famous poem, "Nocturne at Bethesda." We have the theme of

loss—the lost position of the black race in society. This dominant idea is expressed by contrast with man's abandonment of God

The theme is worked out by contrast and by parallel, deftly
moving from a brief sense of hope or relief through salvation
("I thought I saw an angel flying low") to a conclusion that
expresses disappointment. The iambic foundation is jarred
occasionally by a longer or shorter line, as if to emphasize the
black man's sense of loss and dislocation in an alien world. The
poem attains a tone of universality by its paralleling of man's
loss of grace with the sorry lot of the black race. Bontemps
evokes a rich spiritual experience in this poem. When he
abandoned poetry, he deprived the literary world of an authentic Afro-American poetic voice.

Waring Cuney fashioned touching, mildly ironic lines that
carry the weight of their own beauty—a beauty fragile and soft.
He never moved deep into the art and, thus, hard work of
poetry; his verses, a simulacrum of poetic imagination, not of
form, succeed only on a surface level. The just sentiment of
"No Images" anticipates the contemporary concern for recognition of real black beauty:

> She does not know
> Her beauty,
> She thinks her brown body
> Has no glory.
>
> If she could dance
> Naked,
> Under palm trees
> And see her image in the river
> She would know.
>
> But there are no palm trees
> On the street,
> And dishwater gives back no images.[23]

There is an atavistic notion here that does not appear in any of his other poems during this period. Even so, the absorption with beauty in its various guises can be considered one of Cuney's prime concerns.

Cuney's meagre output still reveals enough about his poetry to suggest that it could have been improved if he had been able to objectify his experiences in language that actually revealed his deeply felt interests.[24] Instead, he seems to have remained on the perimeter of his emotions, robbing the reading public of work by someone with minor poetic talent that nevertheless could have enriched the literary world for a longer period of time.

In a recent analysis, Frank Horne's poetry is divided into three major categories; one group, "the quest motif, chiefly in the language of the athletic contest and the planning of a suicide," seems to be arbitrarily determined.[25] Horne, who continued to write poetry until his death in 1974, produced more poetry than most of the minor Harlem Renaissance poets. But it is not easy to classify his poetry aside from the general race consciousness syndrome apparent in most of the serious black poetry of that period. The structure of his poetry derives from his selection of significant moments of pain, joy, and inspiration which he kaleidoscopes in loose, unrhymed, sometimes eliptical phrases. Too often he resorts to clichés: "lips/ Two livid streaks of flame," "dark pool/Of oblivion," and "my heart/A crying thing." But the message, the theme, squirms through, much as the suicide (in "Letters Found Near a Suicide") and "Chick" (to whom one letter is addressed) "slip through/ Fighting and squirming/Over the line/To victory."[26]

There are thirteen poems in the group of "Letters Found Near a Suicide." Each poem is addressed to a person or a group of persons (e.g., "To The Poets"), and we experience the suicide's attempts to understand his past through these last communications. It is as if, in preparing for the death he will deal himself, he wants to prove the necessity of his action by expressing alienation from friends and family. Will everyone, as he writes in "To Wanda," applaud his action, his "last Grand

Gesture?" The alienation and despair, the evocation of the good, clean moments and the bitter ones, are all a part of the mood and tone of these poems.

The texture of the poems is sometimes thin, a fact that is directly related both to his straight, uncomplicated angle of vision and his spare, unadorned language. Horne is clearly a Christian poet as well; he is one who tries to avoid a neat, rigid theological view. He does attempt to enrich his profound beliefs with a more complex vision than unquestioning blind belief allows. For instance, in the last section of his "Letters Found Near a Suicide," entitled "To You," the suicide is addressing Christ in a mildly mocking voice:

All my life
They have told me
That you
Would save my Soul

. . . .

Could be born again. . .

. . . .

You
Who were conceived
Without ecstasy
Or pain

The conceit of the poet is accusatory but, in the last analysis, his argument with Christ is feckless because his use of the birth of Christ never goes beyond one bald statement. Horne does not make use of the complexity of the Virgin Birth (e.g., the varied controversies about the Virgin Birth or the related doctrine of the Immaculate Conception), nor does he terminate this verse (and, thus, the entire group of poems) with any strong impediment to the traditional state of mind of a suicide. To deny God or to minimize the power of the Christian faith (in the poem, obviously Catholic) is not unusual for a suicide; therefore, the closing lines

Can you understand
That I knelt last night
In Your House
And ate Your Body
And drank Your Blood.
. . . and thought only of her?[27]

fail to render the richness of the profound experience Horne
is attempting to enact. "And thought only of her?" shocks the
reader into thinking back on the state of mind and the philosophy
of the suicide. The unexpected mention of "her" causes the
reader to look back at other poems in the series in order to
relate to this unnamed being with a sense of significance. The
nexus does not exist. The attitudes of rejection and alienation
seem to cause the placement of "her" in the last line. This
ambivalent attitude that informs the poem is, of course, a part
of Horne's poetic attempt to display a complexity in his vision
of Christianity. But the ending does not serve the poet or the
poem: the last line has the appearance of being tacked on instead of growing out of the poem; also, the meaning of "her"
is unnecessarily obscure in a poem that has been abundantly
clear up to this point.[28]

Whether by nature or design, it appears that many of the
female poets during this period saw themselves as retainers of
romantic expression. Theirs is a trifling art when read in toto:
too much of the sentiment is transparent; too often what is
expressed is merely sophomoric; far too many of the poems
are simply sentimental verses that should have been left in
private diaries. Romantic poets who happily quote Wordsworth's
notion of poetry as a "spontaneous overflow of powerful feelings" and even as "emotion recollected in tranquility" sometimes overlook this Wordsworthian caveat: "I have never given
way to my own feelings in personifying natural objects . . .
without bringing all that I have said to a rigorous after-test of
good sense."[29]

Georgia Douglas Johnson's poetry has been said to display "delicate lyricism," a description which surely applies to her earlier verses.[30] Johnson's primary concern in poetry is the female self and the emotions that evolve from love, dreams, remembrance, and repression. One poem, "The Heart of a Woman," echoes the feminine plight:

> The heart of woman goes forth with the dawn,
> As a lone bird, soft winging, so restlessly on,
>
> . . . .
>
> The heart of a woman falls back with the night,
> And enters some alien cage in its plight,
> And tries to forget it has dreamed of the stars,
> While it breaks, breaks, breaks on the sheltering bars.[31]

If Johnson had written more in this thematic vein (the verse quality ordinary, even so) she might have avoided some of the sing-song, trifling verses she composed, such as:

> Against the day of sorrow
> Lay by some trifling thing
> A smile, a kiss, a flower
> For sweet remembering.[32]

and:

> The dew is on the grasses, dear,
> The blush is on the rose,
> And swift across our dial-youth,
> A shifting shadow goes.[33]

Johnson was hampered by her paucity of expression, lack of inventiveness with form (there is no apparent attempt, for

instance, to lengthen lines which tend to bog down with mo-
notonous rhythm), and limited ability to see what she is saying.
For instance, she writes: ‹

> I am folding up my little dreams
> Within my heart tonight,[34]

ignoring the absolutely unoriginal, failed metaphor. Another
poem states:

> I left my lagging heart outside
> Within the dark alone,
> I heard it singing through the gloom
> A wordless, anguished tone.[35]

In the imprecision of "a wordless, anguished tone," the poet
risks appearing silly instead of sensitive.

Johnson's concern with racial matters, in such poems as
"The Suppliant," "Interracial," "Common Dust," and "Old
Black Men" links her with the Harlem Renaissance. Despite her
easy sentimentalism, she was probably deeply moved when
writing her love lyrics (e.g., "I Want to Die While You Love
Me," and "Remember"), and she was not alone in writing this
type of poem. She was merely less successful and less satisfy-
ing with her love lyrics than, for instance, Cullen. But she was,
after all, a product of a time (she was born in 1886) when the
polite black bourgeois woman was praised for writing sentimental, sensitive-sounding verse. She had three volumes of
poetry published during the Harlem Renaissance period, a noteworthy feat in itself.[36]

Gwendolyn Bennett's poetry, highly emotional and intense,
is marked by attempts to soar. A strong sense of racial attachment is evident as well, such as in "Hermitage":

> I want to see the slim palm trees,
> Pulling at the clouds
> With little pointed fingers. . . .
> I want to see lithe Negro girls,
> Etched dark against the sky
> While sunset lingers.[37]

Her poem, "Lines Written at the Grave of Alexandre Dumas" is not in this genre; instead, it is a lament for "hearts with shattered loves."

Bennett has a strong penchant for personification: "Night wears a garment/All velvet soft, all violet blue . . . " ("Street Lamps in Early Spring"[38]); "He bent to kiss and raised his visor's lace . . . /All eager-lipped I kissed the mouth of death" ("Sonnet I"[39]); "Memory will lay its hands/Upon your breast . . ." (Hatred[40]). The device, however, does not suceed because the poems in which they appear are romantically puerile.

In the poem, "Sonnet II," Bennett nearly sustains the thought pattern, even when resorting to clichés (e.g., "flowers bathed by rain," "winds that sing among the trees"), but her last fails because she succumbs to bathos:

> But dearer far than all surmise
> Are sudden tear-drops in your eyes.[41]

Years later, Jacques Prévert wrote the same sort of poem and carried it off simply because the last line grew out of the preceding ones. Bennett's terminating line exemplifies the banal sentimentalism, racial or romantic, present in many poems written by blacks in this period. When Bennett draws away from romance and its effects, she does manage to build images and a clear line of thought that help to shape an integrated work as opposed to rambling bursts of sentiment. "Heritage" and "To a Dark Girl," for instance, are better poems because Bennett put herself at a little distance from the central idea without sacrificing the emotion of commitment to her African heritage.

That most uncritical of critics, Benjamin Brawley, aptly says of Anne Spencer:

> [She] has an independent and compressed style of writing that makes special appeal to the intelligent. There is hardly any reference to race at all in her poems; instead there is sometimes an exotic note, as in 'Before the Feast of Shushan.' She shows a preference for modern verse-forms and never leaves one in doubt as to her command of her medium.[42]

The editors of *The Negro Caravan* note: "Her poetry is closer to the metaphysical than that of any other American Negro poet. . . . Anne Spencer is an individualist."[43]

Spencer produced good minor poems that reflect an ordered intellect. In her poem, "Life-long, Poor Browning," she gives honor to her beloved home-state, Virginia, and a tribute to Browning with visual and sensual accuracy. Her lines have beauty, vigor, and even a touch of lightness (a little Browningesque energy, perhaps):

> Life-long, poor Browning never knew Virginia
> Or he'd not grieved in Florence for April sallies
> Back to English gardens after Euclid's linear:
> Clipt yews, Pomander Walks, and pleached alleys.

The very use of "pleached," for instance, instead of plaited or braided (to draw closer to a black-oriented description) reveals an inventive, yet careful, writer. Near the end of the poem she describes nature as one who is intimate with its actual gifts (and throws in a successful slanted rhyme):

Here canopied reaches of dogwood and hazel,
Beech tree and redbud fine-laced in vines,
Fleet clapping rills by lush fern and basil,
Drain blue hills to lowlands scented with pines.[44]

Spencer's indebtedness to nature is sensitively combined with a conventional reminiscence about love in "Lines to a Nasturtium":

A bird, next, small and humming,
Looked into your startled depths and fled . . .
Surely, some dread sight, and dafter
Than human eyes as mine can see,
Set the stricken air waves drumming
In his flight.[45]

. . . .

Hands like, how like, brown lillies sweet,
Cloth of gold were fair enough to touch her feet . . . .
Ah, how the senses flood at my repeating,
As once in her fire-lit heart I felt the furies
Beating, beating.[46]

In "For Jim, Easter Eve," she draws a careful analogy between a lover's hurt and the Agony in the Garden of Gethsemane. In a melodic fashion she both attenuates and makes the emotion expand gradually in order to give profundity to a deeply felt experience:

Lacking old tombs, here stands my grief,
and certainly its ancient tree.
Peace is here and in every season
a quiet beauty.
The sky falling about me
evenly to the compass . . .

What is sorrow but tenderness now
in this earth-close frame of land and sky
falling constantly into horizons
of east and west, north and south.[47]

In a complex of images, Spencer weaves a poem, "At the
Carnival," that explores innocence, beauty, despair, and belief.[48] The narrator, in a depressed mood, feels that "the color
of life was gray." But the "gay little Girl-of-the-Diving-Tank"
is pure and beautiful and may save those about her from their
impurity, brooding, and enchainment. The girl might also fall
prey to the human failings of those about her; therefore, the
poet says, "I implore Neptune to claim his child today."[49] The
descriptions and musings in the poem are deft and strong in
their visual linguistics. For instance, of the diving girl, the poet
writes, "Innocence is its own adoring." The place itself and a
lewd dancer are pictured thus:

Here the sausage and garlic booth
Sent unholy incense skyward;
There a quivering female-thing
Gestured assignations, and lied
To call it dancing.[50]

The observations and the sustained tone of the poem make it
an uncommonly good example of what can be accomplished
in the genre.

Spencer produced a small amount of poetry, however, in
comparison with the quantities of verse written and published
by Cullen, McKay, and Hughes. This possibly stems from the
exquisite vision of her poetic mind which seems to possess a
private, insular quality. Amazingly, Spencer ignored the more
sentimental aspects of race, religion, and romance. This omission

may account for the fact that her poetry can be considered superior to that of the other minor poets of the Harlem Renaissance

In her poems about love and race, Helene Johnson exhibits
more emotional control than either Gwendolyn Bennett or
Georgia Douglas Johnson. The fact that Helene Johnson was
the youngest of these minor poets may account for this absence
of overriding sentimentalism and artificial expression.

In the poem, "Fulfillment," which won First Honorable
Mention in the 1926 *Opportunity* contest, Helene Johnson, at
the age of nineteen, demonstrates her grasp of form and her
conscious striving to break away from clichés.[51] There are
jejune poetic phrases such as "pregnant earth," "strong tree's
bosom," and "Ah, life, to let your stabbing beauty pierce me";
but there are also original, striking metaphors that show promise: "a patent-leathered Negro," "the rain drool," and the rain,
again, that splashes "with a wet giggle." Earlier that year, a
poem of hers that was all metaphor, "Night," was printed; it
was not strong or deep verse, but it revealed a writer of above-
ordinary talent.

There is an earthy, full quality in Johnson's poems, as well
as imagery that is flighty and romantic. Her heart is in the soul
of her people; in her efforts to recreate the special quality of
blackness, she anticipates the move away from traditional
poetic forms that contemporary black poets have found so
confining. "Magalu" moves into the primordial African homeland that symbolizes freedom for the black man:

> I met Magalu, dark as a tree at night,
> Eager-lipped, listening to a man with a white collar
>
> Do not let him lure you from your laughing waters,
> Lulling lakes, lissome winds.
> Would you sell the colors of your sunset and the fragrance
> Of your flowers, and the passionate wonder of your forest
> For a creed that will not let you dance?[52]

The poem has Whitmanesque vigor and assertiveness. There is also a touch of womanly softness that imbues it with dark sensuousness.

Johnson's preoccupation with her race and its struggles is pithily expressed in "The Road." Some of her bitterness about racism is found in the cynical poem, "Fiat Lux," a poem about a black woman in jail.[53] But she is best when summoning up the image of the uncontained, urban Negro who has, deep-down, the stirrings of his native roots (soul):

> Gee, brown boy, i loves you all over.
> I'm glad I'm a jig. I'm glad I can
> Understand your dancin' and your
> Singin', and feel all the happiness
> And joy, and don't-care in you.
> Gee, boy, when you sing, I can close my ears
> And hear tom-toms just as plain.[54]

In "Sonnet to a Negro in Harlem," she uses this conventional, restrictive verse form to show scorn for what white America has tried to do to blacks:

> You are disdainful and magnificent—
> Your perfect body and your pompous gait,
> Your dark eyes flashing solemnly with hate,
> Small wonder that you are incompetent
> To imitate those whom you so despise—
> Your shoulders towering high above the throng,
> Your head thrown back in rich, barbaric song,
> Palm trees and mangoes stretched before your eyes.[55]

Johnson's strong identification with her racial antecedents and her avoidance of some of the more blatant defects such as excessive clichés, misfired metaphors, and extravagant sentiments permitted her to write some quite commendable poems.

She seemed to long for the unshackled truth, for the sort of freedom that would allow her to embrace life in the present, the past, and the future, as voiced, in a fashion, in her poem, "Invocation":

And do not keep my plot mowed smooth
And clean as a spinster's bed,
But let the weed, the flower, the tree,
Riotous, rampant, wild and free,
Grow high above my head.[56]

These minor black poets, in addition to thematic concerns, shared several features with their better-known, more productive black poetic brethren. There was, first of all, an absence (Sterling Brown excepted) of dialect verse. The use of metaphor became more sophisticated, even when it was employed, as was frequently true, for images that were overworked (e.g., metaphors of blackness). On the other hand, this poetry, much of it growing from the oral folk tradition, metaphorically announced an end to or lessening of the need to employ the "double-meaning" language that enriched the common Negro folk tale. Closely allied with the preoccupation with their race or racial heritage was a faint glimmer of independence from the values of Western civilization. This resulted in a touch of exoticism and reliance on invoking Africa primarily for an effect rather than for enlarging on a deeply felt emotion. There was also a genteelness in the poetry, especially in versification forms and metrics, as if these poets were in the midst of the Victorian era instead of being surrounded by men and women who were fashioning brilliant poetry in modern idioms.

If literary art were measured by the strongest features and the best examples of its practitioners, the reader would be robbed of balance and range in literature. Therefore, the question of why one ought to examine, even in the briefest manner, the minor writers of a group that, in itself, was minor in a period when major modern writers were developing is partially answered. If an effort towards inclusiveness is not excuse enough, one might also consider the loss of not learning about writers who sensed that they were part of a movement that was variously termed the Harlem Renaissance, Negro Renaissance, or the period of the New Negro. These writers were there in time if not always in place (Anne Spencer, for instance, did not leave her native Virginia, but she was known by other Harlem Renaissance writers). These poets (and others not examined, such as Frank Marshall Davis and Angelina Grimké) were competing against Cullen, Hughes, and McKay in the buyers' market. Not to be exposed to the best of Bontemps, to miss the sonority of *God's Trombones* (which makes a bid for being a major work of the Harlem Renaissance), or to forget the sensitive, probing poetry of Spencer is reason enough to note what these and other minor poets offered.

NOTES

1. James Weldon Johnson, *Along This Way* (New York: Viking, c. 1961, c. 1933), p. 377.

2. James Weldon Johnson, *God's Trombones; Seven Negro Sermons in Verse* (New York: Viking, c. 1955, c. 1927), p. 27.

3. Johnson, *Along This Way*, p. 377.

4. Ibid., p. 378.

5. Johnson, *God's Trombones*, p. 10.

6. Ibid., pp. 48-49.

7. Johnson, *Along This Way*, p. 336.

8. Johnson, *God's Trombones*, p. 30.

9. Ibid., pp. 41-42.

10. Ibid., p. 9.

11. Rayford Logan, editor, *The New Negro Thirty Years Afterwards* (Washington, D.C.: Howard University Press, 1955), p. 57.

12. Sterling A. Brown, *Southern Road* (New York: Harcourt, Brace, 1932), pp. 14, 15-16.

13. Alain Locke, "Sterling Brown: The New Negro Folk-Poet." In Nancy Cunard, editor, *Negro, An Anthology* (New York: Frederick Ungar, c. 1970), p. 90.

14. Jean Wagner, *Black Poets of the United States from Paul Laurence Dunbar to Langston Hughes* (Urbana: University of Illinois Press, 1973), p. 477.

15. Brown, *Southern Road*, p. 73.

16. Ibid., p. xv.

17. Ibid., pp. 83-84.

18. Ibid., p. 53.

19. Aime Césaire, *Cahier d'un Retour au Pays Natal* (n.p.: Presence Africaine, 1968), p. 100. Translation in this edition (p. 101) is: "My Negritude is neither a tower nor a cathedral/it thrusts into the red flesh of the soil."

20. Langston Hughes and Arna Bontemps, editors, *Poetry of the Negro, 1746-1949* (Garden City: Doubleday, 1949), p. 215.

21. Ibid., p. 216.

22. Ibid., p. 225.

23. Arna Bontemps, *American Negro Poetry* (New York: Hill and Wang, 1974), p. 98.

24. Cuney did write verses in the 1930s—propagandistic and not very distinguished.

25. Ronald Primeau, "Frank Horne and the Second Echelon Poets." In Arna Bontemps, editor, *The Harlem Renaissance Remembered* (New York: Dodd, 1972), p. 248.

26. Bontemps, *American Negro Poetry*, p. 44. Title here is "Notes Found Near a Suicide" instead of "Letters . . . "

27. Ibid., p. 50.

28. A discussion of the meaning of "her" is in the essay by Primeau ("Frank Horne and the Second Echelon Poets," p. 254).

29. Wordsworth to W. R. Hamilton, 23 December 1829, in Ernest de Selincourt, editor, *The Letters of William and Dorothy Wordsworth; The Later Years,* I (Oxford: Clarendon Press, 1939), pp. 436-437.

30. *The Negro Caravan*, p. 279.

31. Hughes and Bontemps, *Poetry of the Negro*, p. 73.

32. Bontemps, *American Negro Poetry*, p. 21.

33. Hughes and Bontemps, *Poetry of the Negro*, p. 74.

34. Ibid., p. 81.

35. Ibid., p. 79.

36. Ibid., p. 612.

37. Bontemps, *American Negro Poetry*, pp. 73-74.

38. *Opportunity* 4 (May 1926): 152.

39. Bontemps, *American Negro Poetry*, p. 75.

40. Ibid., p. 73.

41. Ibid., p. 75.

42. Benjamin Brawley, *The Negro Genius; a New Appraisal of the Achievement of the American Negro in Literature and the Fine Arts* (New York: Dodd, 1937), pp. 229-230.

43. *The Negro Caravan*, p. 281.

44. Hughes and Bontemps, *Poetry of the Negro*, p. 60.

45. Ibid., p. 54.

46. Ibid.

47. Ibid., pp. 54-55.

48. Ibid., p. 52.

49. Ibid., p. 53.

50. Ibid.

51. *Opportunity* 4 (June 1926): 194.

52. Hughes and Bontemps, *Poetry of the Negro*, p. 263.

53. *The Messenger* 8 (July 1926): 199.

54. Bontemps, *American Negro Poetry*, p. 101.

55. Ibid., p. 102.

56. Ibid.

EPILOGUE

The Harlem Renaissance. What was it? What did it mean?

The expanded decade of the 1920s was in part paradise, in part hell for the black literary intellectuals who were attempting to define themselves through their art. The Harlem Renaissance period, then, was first of all a highly self-conscious time for the black writer. The Great War had just ended; it was a propitious time to strike for a new beginning in America. The New Negro arose. Second, many began to search for the meaning of the black heritage, the significance of what the American Negro had inherited from his spiritual and cultural past. There was, third, a yearning to assert black values without distortion. For a people not quite sure of having a group spirit (and Claude McKay was quick to say that this was just the trouble), the task was insurmountable. But what it amounted to was a frenetic scrambling to produce a corrected image of blackness. If one can say that these intellectuals failed because they did not formulate a "cultural philosophy," one can also say they succeeded because no one seems able to pinpoint precisely what they did achieve.[1] The tolerant, sympathetic critic can share Nathan Huggins's conclusion: "Whatever else, the era produced a phenomenal race consciousness and race assertion, as well as unprecedented numbers of poems, stories, and works of art by black people."[2] The less sympathetic critic can take the viewpoint of Harold Cruse, who faults the Harlem Renaissance for its lack of focus, its (to use his precise term) "inspired aimlessness."[3] In the literary sphere, certainly, there was perplexity about the proper stance to adopt. There was Cullen, contradicting himself about the importance of race in his writing, who was seen as a true aesthete; there was DuBois who without hesitation said that "all art is propaganda"; there was McKay, a gentle radical who wandered about the world seeking truth and peace, a poet quite possibly best described by himself: "For I was born, far from my native clime,/ Under the white man's menace, out of time"; there was Thurman, psychologically and emotionally insecure, intellectually trenchant, cynical because he and his friends could not live up to the promise of their decade; and there was Hughes, never revealing what lay hidden below that charming, folksy fellow who published what could have become the black writer's manifesto: "We younger Negro artists who create now intend to express our individual dark-skinned selves without fear or shame. . . . We build our temples for tomorrow, strong as we know how, and we stand on top of the mountain, free within ourselves."[4] But, of course, he was speaking only for himself and a handful of other writers who managed to shock the black bourgeoisie and titillate white voyeurs.

What we have, then, are works without a single faith, works accomplished in the sweat of self-discovery or self-searching or simply self-delusion. The controlling symbol, presaging a portion of Négritude, was expressed variously but centered rather consistently on the primary idea of blackness—the importance of this very fact of the artist's current life and the heritage deriving from the African genesis. In the New World, the symbol and reservoir for this heritage and its accumulated culture was the black capital of the nation, Harlem. As symbol and reality it operated as a source of inspiration. The writers hopped all around the United States and Europe; yet, in a sense, they drew strength from the knowledge that this one place was the black man's home.

Cruse's thesis-accusation is partially valid, especially in hindsight. Indeed, the inchoate movement was unfocused in historical terms. What does this mean? The members of the movement wanted to believe in their own immortality and suspected the route lay somewhere between uniqueness (i.e., being black, sounding black) and conformity to an obscure norm. In succumbing to the neuroticism of this "twoness" that DuBois speaks of, the black writer anesthetized himself to many of the gifts of the cultural past he was extolling. It was a phony paean to the past, but the writer was not always aware that this was so. To understand one's own period is to be a philosopher, part historian, part poet, part seer. Thurman, without compassion, saw the faults that they all shared; later, Locke was to experience a portion of this same disillusionment. The peculiar problem of the black writer during this period in American literary history was how to incorporate his African heritage (What was it? How did it make him "different?" How does one dramatize this difference?) and his American heritage into a distinct Afro-American literature. The tools, after all, were the English language and English versification and prose forms, which they did not choose to repudiate. To remold these supposedly alien devices was the issue, but they never resolved it. James Weldon Johnson attempted to circumvent it in *God's Trombones*; Sterling Brown, spurning the niceties Johnson recognized (white readership, for one thing), reverted to the dialect language and perhaps came closest to unravelling the psychological-artistic wrangling in which his fellow-writers were engaged in their search for an authentic Afro-American literary voice.

It happened, in any case. Call it the Negro Renaissance, the Harlem Movement, the New Negro Movement, or the Harlem Renaissance—it happened in time and, partially, in place. Years after it was over, Dorothy West reflected: "It [Thurman's death] was the first break in the ranks of the 'New Negro.' They assembled in solemn silence, older, hardly wiser, and reminded for the first time of their lack of immortality."[5]

Not immortal? Who is to say?

"The golden days were gone. Or was it just the bloom of youth that had been lost?"[6]

NOTES

1. Harold Cruse, *The Crisis of the Negro Intellectual* (New York: Morrow, c. 1971), p. 38.

2. Nathan Irvin Huggins, *Harlem Renaissance* (New York: Oxford, 1971), p. 83.

3. Cruse, *The Crisis of the Negro Intellectual*, p. 37.

4. Langston Hughes, "The Negro Artist and the Racial Mountain," *The Nation* 122 (23 June 1926): 694.

5. Dorothy West, "Elephant's Dance; a Memoir of Wallace Thurman," *Black World* 20 (November 1970): 85.

6. Arna Bontemps, "The Awakening: A Memoir." In Arna Bontemps, editor, *The Harlem Renaissance Remembered* (New York: Dodd, Mead, 1972), p. 26.

APPENDIX

APPENDIX : CHRONOLOGY

YEAR	MAJOR PUBLICATIONS/ PLAYS/MUSICALS	EVENTS/DEATHS	Lynchings Black	Lynchings White	MISCELLANEA Other Items
1917	Millay-*Renascence. . .* Great Negro migration (1916-1919) Bolshevik Revolution in Russia U.N.I.A. founded (Garvey)	U.S. enters WWI (6 April)	36	2	1st awarding of Pulitzer Prize
1918	Adams-*Education of Henry Adams* Cather-*My Antonia* Joyce-*Ulysses* (parts) in *Little Review*	Walter White joins NAACP staff	60	4	
1919	Anderson-*Winesburg, Ohio* Cabell-*Jurgen* McKay-"If we must die" in *The Liberator* Reed-*Ten Days That Shook the World*	Versailles Peace Conference Prohibition Amendment (18th) adopted 1 January 1920 Race riots American Legion founded Ku Klux Klan reactivated	76	7	
1920	DuBois-*Darkwater* Lewis-*Main Street* O'Neill-*Emperor Jones* Wharton-*Age of Innocence*	Warren Harding elected to presidency Right-to-vote for women (19th Amendment)	53	8	Negro population: 10,463,131 (9.9%) Beginning of commercial radio broadcasting
1921	Dos Passos-*Three Soldiers* Johnson-*Book of American Negro Poetry* Sissle-Blake musical, "Shuffle Along" Gilpin in "Emperor Jones" (play)	Tulsa race riots Sacco and Vanzetti accused of murder	59	5	
1922	Cummings-*Enormous Room* Eliot-*Waste Land*	Mussolini becomes dictator of Italy	51	6	"Shuffle Along" comes to Broadway

continued on following page

MAJOR PUBLICATIONS/PLAYS/MUSICALS   EVENTS/DEATHS   MISCELLANEA

YEAR	MAJOR PUBLICATIONS/PLAYS/MUSICALS	EVENTS/DEATHS	Lynchings Black	Lynchings White	Other Items
	Joyce-Ulysses Lewis-Babbitt McKay-Harlem Shadows				
1923	Stevens-Harmonium Toomer-Cane	Hitler's abortive "Beerhall Putsch," Munich Teapot Dome scandal (1923-1924)	29	4	Opportunity: Journal of Negro Life begins publication
1924	Fauset-There Is Confusion White-Fire in the Flint	Coolidge elected to presidency Lenin's death	16	0	Opportunity prizes for creative expression announced
1925	Cullen-Color Dos Passos-Manhattan Transfer Dreiser-American Tragedy Eliot-Poems, 1909-1925 Fitzgerald-Great Gatsby Glasgow-Barren Ground H.D.-Collected Poems Hemingway-In Our Time Jeffers-Roan Stallion Lewis-Arrowsmith Locke-New Negro	Scopes trial, Dayton, Tenn. Garvey imprisoned	17	0	Guggenheim Fellowships begun Thurman arrives in New York City
1926	Hemingway-Sun Also Rises Hughes-Weary Blues Waldrond-Tropic Death White-Flight "The Blackbirds of 1926" (Florence Mills in this musical show)		23	7	

1927	Cather-*Death Comes for the Archbishop* Cullen-*Ballad of the Brown Girl* Cullen-*Copper Sun* Hemingway-*Men Without Women* Hughes-*Fine Clothes to the Jew* Johnson, C.-*Ebony & Topaz* Johnson, J.W.-*God's Trombones* Parrington-*Main Currents in American Thought* vols. I-II Robinson-*Tristam* Wilder-*Bridge of San Luis Rey*	Sacco and Vanzetti executed Lindbergh's nonstop flight to Paris Garvey deported Florence Mills's death Clarissa Scott Delany's death	16	0
1928	Benet-*John Brown's Body* DuBois-*Dark Princess* Fauset-*Plum Bun* Fisher-*Walls of Jericho* Larsen-*Quicksand* McKay-*Home to Harlem* O'Neill-*Strange Interlude*	Trotsky and followers exiled from Russia Paris Peace Pact (Kellogg-Briand)	10	1	Oscar De Priest becomes the first Negro congressman from a Northern state
1929	Cullen-*Black Christ* Faulkner-*Sound and the Fury* Faulkner-*Sartoris* Hemingway-*Farewell to Arms* Lewis-*Dodsworth* McKay-*Banjo* Rice-*Street Scene* Thurman-*Blacker the Berry* Wolfe-*Look Homeward Angel*	Collapse of New York Stock Market	7	3
1930	Connelly-*Green Pastures* Crane-*The Bridge* Dos Passos-*42nd Parallel* Eliot-*Ash Wednesday*		20	1	Sinclair Lewis receives Nobel Prize

continued on following page

MAJOR PUBLICATIONS/   EVENTS/DEATHS   MISCELLANEA

YEAR	MAJOR PUBLICATIONS/PLAYS/MUSICALS	EVENTS/DEATHS	Lynchings Black	White	Other Items
1931	Faulkner-*As I Lay Dying* Hughes-*Not Without Laughter* Porter-*Flowering Judas*	Invasion of Manchuria by Japan Scottsboro Trial Spanish Revolution	12	1	
	Bontemps-*God Sends Sunday* Buck-*Good Earth* Cather-*Shadows on the Rock* Faulkner-*Sanctuary* Fauset-*Chinaberry Tree* O'Neill-*Mourning Becomes Electra* Wilson-*Axel's Castle*				
1932	Brown-*Southern Road* Cullen-*One Way to Heaven* Dos Passos-*1919* Farrell-*Young Lonigan* Faulkner-*Light in August* Fisher-*Conjure-man Dies* McKay-*Gingertown* Thurman-*Infants of the Spring*	FDR defeats Hoover for the presidency Lindbergh kidnapping case Scottsboro case before the Supreme Court Death of Chesnutt	6	2	
1933	Fauset-*Comedy, American Style* McKay-*Banana Bottom* Stein-*Autobiography of Alice B. Toklas*	First Scottsboro trials Hitler becomes chancellor FDR inaugurated as 32nd president Repeal of Prohibition	24	4	
1934	Hurston-*Jonah's Gourd Vine*	Deaths of Rudolph Fisher and Wallace Thurman	15	0	

BIBLIOGRAPHY

GENERAL BOOKS AND ARTICLES

Page numbers are not given for those books that deal with the Harlem Renaissance in a partial manner.

Bercovici, Konrad. "The Black Blocks of Manhattan." *Harpers Monthly Magazine* 149 (1924): 613-623.

Berry, Faith. "Voices for the Jazz Age, Great Migration or Black Bourgeoisie." *Black World*, November 1970, pp. 10-16.

Black World, November 1970. This whole issue is devoted to the Harlem Renaissance.

Bland, Edward. "Racial Bias and Negro Poetry." *Poetry* 63 (1944): 328-333.

———. "Social Forces Shaping the Negro Novel." *The Negro Quarterly* 1 (1942): 241-248.

Bone, Robert A. *The Negro Novel in America*. Rev. ed. New Haven: Yale University Press, 1965.

Bontemps, Arna. "The Black Renaissance of the Twenties." *Black World*, November 1970, pp. 5-9.

———, ed. *The Harlem Renaissance Remembered.* New York: Dodd, Mead, 1972.

Braithwaite, William Stanley. "Alain Locke's Relationship to the Negro in American Literature." *Phylon* 18 (1957): 166-173.

Brawley, Benjamin. "The Negro Literary Renaissance." *Southern Workman* 56 (1927): 177-184.

Brown, Sterling A. *Negro Poetry and Drama.* Washington, D.C.: Associates in Negro Folk Education, 1937.

Carrington, Glenn. "The Harlem Renaissance—A Personal Memoir." *Freedomways* 3 (1963): 307-311.

Chapman, Abraham. "The Harlem Renaissance in Literary History." *CLA Journal* 11 (1967): 38-58.

Clarke, John Henrik. "The Neglected Dimensions of the Harlem Renaissance." *Black World*, November 1970, pp. 118-129.

Coleman, Leon Duncan. "The Contribution of Carl Van Vechten to the Negro Renaissance; 1920-1930." Ph.D. dissertation, University of Minnesota, 1969.

Collier, Eugenia W. "Heritage from Harlem," *Black World*, November 1970, pp. 52-59.

Cruse, Harold. *The Crisis of the Negro Intellectual.* New York: William Morrow, 1967.

Fisher, Rudolph. "The Caucasian Storms Harlem." *The American Mercury* 11 (1927): 393-398.

Fox, R. M. "The Negro Renaissance." [London] *Labour Magazine* (1928): 306-308.

Gloster, Hugh M. *Negro Voices in American Fiction.* Chapel Hill: University of North Carolina Press, 1948.

Gruening, Martha. "The Negro Renaissance." *Hound and Horn* 5 (1932): 504-514.

Hart, Robert C. "Black-White Literary Relations in the Harlem Renaissance." *American Literature* 44 (1973): 612-628.

Huggins, Nathan Irvin. *Harlem Renaissance.* New York: Oxford University Press, 1971.

Hughes, Langston. *The Big Sea, An Autobiography.* New York: Hill and Wang, 1963, c. 1940.

———. "Harlem Literati in the Twenties." *The Saturday Review*, 22 June 1940, pp. 13-14.

———. "The Twenties: Harlem and Its Negritude." *African Forum* 1 (1966): 11-20.

Jackson, Augusta V. "The Renascence of Negro Literature, 1922-1929." Master's thesis, Atlanta University, 1936.

Johnson, James Weldon. *Black Manhattan*. New Preface by Allan H. Spear. New York: Atheneum, 1968.

———. "The Making of Harlem" *Survey Graphic* 53 (1925): 635-639.

Keller, Frances Richardson. "The Harlem Renaissance." *North American Review* 253 (1968): 29-34.

Killens, John O. "Another Time When Black Was Beautiful." *Black World*, November 1970, pp. 20-36.

Locke, Alain. "Harlem." *Survey Graphic* 53 (1925): 629-630. (Part of this same essay appears in *The New Negro.)*

———, ed. *The New Negro: An Interpretation.* New York: Albert and Charles Boni, 1925.

Lomax, Michael L. "Fantasies of Affirmation: The 1920's Novel of Negro Life." *CLA Journal* 16 (1972): 232-246.

Lueders, Edward. *Carl Van Vechten and the Twenties*. Albuquerque: University of New Mexico Press, 1955.

Moore, Gerald. "Poetry in the Harlem Renaissance." In *The Black American Writer*, vol. 2, edited by C.W.E. Bigsby, pp. 67-76. Baltimore: Penguin Books, 1969.

Morris, Lloyd. "The Negro 'Renaissance.' " *Southern Workman* 59 (1930): 82-86.

Sklar, Robert, ed. *The Plastic Age (1917-1930).* New York: George Braziller, 1970.

Taussig, Charlotte E. "The New Negro as Revealed in His Poetry." *Opportunity* 5 (1927): 108-111.

Thorpe, Earl E. *The Mind of the Negro: An Intellectual History of Afro-Americans*. Baton Rouge: Ortlieb Press, 1961.

Thurman, Wallace. "Negro Life in New York's Harlem: A Lively Picture of a Popular and Interesting Section." *Haldeman-Julius Quarterly* [no vol. no.] (1924): 132-145.

———. "Nephews of Uncle Remus." *The Independent* 119 (1927): 296-298. (Although the article is brief, the author manages to discuss Cullen, Fisher, Johnson, and Toomer.)

Vincent, Theodore G., ed. *Voices of a Black Nation: Political Journalism in the Harlem Renaissance.* San Francisco: Ramparts Press, 1973.

Waldrond, Eric D. "The Black City." *The Messenger* 6 (1924): 13-14.

Williams, John A. "The Harlem Renaissance: Its Artists, Its Impact, Its Meaning." *Black World,* November 1970, pp. 17-18.

BOOKS AND ARTICLES ABOUT SPECIFIC AUTHORS

Some of the items included in this section may have appeared in Part I also. Articles or books that apply to more than one author will appear as applicable to specific authors. This arrangement is purely personal, based on the author's inclination to have as much information close at hand as possible.

BROWN, STERLING A. (1901-)

Collier, Eugenia W. "I Do Not marvel, Countee Cullen." *CLA Journal* 11 (1967): 73-87.

Ford, Nick Aaron. "The Negro Author's Use of Propaganda in Imaginative Literature." Ph.D. dissertation, State University of Iowa, 1945.

Jackson, Blyden and Louis Rubin. *Black Poetry in America.* Baton Rouge: Louisiana State University Press, 1974.

Killens, John O. "Another Time When Black Was Beautiful." *Black World,* November 1970, pp. 20-36.

Wagner, Jean. *Black Poets of the United States from Paul Laurence Dunbar to Langston Hughes.* Urbana: University of Illinois Press, 1973.

CULLEN, COUNTEE (1903-1946)

Arden, Eugene. "The Early Harlem Novel." *Phylon* 20 (1959): 25-31.

Bontemps, Arna, ed. *The Harlem Renaissance Remembered.* New York: Dodd, Mead, 1972.

Bronz, Stephen H. *Roots of Negro Racial Consciousness; the 1920's: Three Harlem Renaissance Authors.* New York: Libra Publishers, 1964.

Christian, Barbara. "Spirit Bloom in Harlem: The Search for a Black Aesthetic During the Harlem Renaissance; the Poetry of Claude McKay, Countee Cullen, and Jean Toomer." Ph.D. dissertation, Columbia University, 1970.

Collier, Eugenia W. "I Do Not Marvel, Countee Cullen." *CLA Journal* 11 (1967): 73-87.

Davis, Arthur P. *From the Dark Tower; Afro-American Writers 1900-1960.* Washington. D.C.: Howard University Press, 1974.

Ford, Nick Aaron. "The Negro Author's Use of Propaganda in Imaginative Literature." Ph.D. dissertation, State University of Iowa, 1945.

Gloster, Hugh M. *Negro Voices in American Fiction.* Chapel Hill: University of North Carolina Press, 1948.

Hansell, William Harold. "Positive Themes in the Poetry of Four Negroes: Claude McKay, Countée Cullen, Langston Hughes, and Gwendolyn Brooks." Ph.D. dissertation, University of Wisconsin, 1972.

Isaacs, Harold R. "Five Writers and Their African Ancestors." *Phylon* 21 (1960): 243-265.

Jackson, Blyden and Louis Rubin. *Black Poetry in America.* Baton Rouge: Louisiana State University Press, 1974.

Lederer, Richard. "The Didactic and the Literary in Four Harlem Renaissance Sonnets." *English Journal* 62 (1973): 219-223.

Moore, Gerald. "Poetry in the Harlem Renaissance. In *The Black American Writer*, vol. 2, edited by C.W.E. Bigsby, pp. 67-76. Baltimore: Penguin Books, 1969.

Perry, Margaret. *A Bio-Bibliography of Countee P. Cullen, 1903-1946.* Westport, Conn.: Greenwood Publishing Co., 1971.

Shucard, Alan Robert. "The Poetry of Countée P. Cullen." Ph.D. dissertation, University of Arizona, 1971.

Starke, Catherine Juanita. *Black Portraiture in American Fiction: Stock Characters, Archetypes, and Individuals.* New York: Basic Books, 1971.

Turner, Darwin T. *In a Minor Chord: Three Afro-American Writers and Their Search for Identity.* Carbondale: Southern Illinois University Press, 1971.

Wagner, Jean. *Black Poets of the United States from Paul Laurence Dunbar to Langston Hughes.* Urbana: University of Illinois Press, 1973.

FAUSET, JESSIE REDMOND (1885?-1961)

Bontemps, Arna, ed. *The Harlem Renaissance Remembered.* New York: Dodd, Mead, 1972.

Braithwaite, William Stanley. "The Novels of Jessie Fauset." *Opportunity* 12 (1934): 24-28.

Ford, Nick Aaron. "The Negro Author's Use of Propaganda in Imaginative
      Literature." Ph.D. dissertation, State University of Iowa, 1945.
Gloster, Hugh M. *Negro Voices in American Fiction*. Chapel Hill: Univer-
      sity of North Carolina Press, 1948.
Gruening, Martha. "The Negro Renaissance." *Hound and Horn* 5 (1932):
      504-514.
Starkey, Marion L. "Jessie Fauset." *Southern Workman* 61 (1932): 218-
      219.

FISHER, RUDOLPH (1897-1934)

Ford, Nick Aaron. "The Negro Author's Use of Propaganda in Imagina-
      tive Literature." Ph.D. dissertation. State University of Iowa, 1945.
Davis, Arthur P. *From the Dark Tower: Afro-American Writers 1900-
      1960*. Washington, D.C.: Howard University Press, 1974.
Gloster, Hugh M. *Negro Voices in American Fiction*. Chapel Hill: Univer-
      sity of North Carolina Press, 1948.
Turpin, Waters E. "Four Short Fiction Writers of the Harlem Renais-
      sance—Their Legacy of Achievement." *CLA Journal* 11 (1967):
      59-72.

HUGHES, LANGSTON (1902-1967)

Barisonzi, Judith Anne. "Black Identity in the Poetry of Langston
      Hughes." Ph.D. dissertation, University of Wisconsin, 1971.
Bontemps, Arna, ed. *The Harlem Renaissance Remembered*. New York:
      Dodd, Mead, 1972.
Davis, Arthur P. *From the Dark Tower: Afro-American Writers 1900-
      1960*. Washington, D.C.: Howard University Press, 1974.
Dickinson, Donald C. *A Bio-Bibliography of Langston Hughes, 1902-
      1967*. Hamden, Conn.: Archon, 1967.
Ford, Nick Aaron. "The Negro Author's Use of Propaganda in Imagina-
      tive Literature." Ph.D. dissertation, State University of Iowa, 1945.
Gibson, Donald B., ed. *Five Black Writers*. New York: New York Univer-
      sity Press, 1970.
Gloster, Hugh M. *Negro Voices in American Fiction*. Chapel Hill: Univer-
      sity of North Carolina Press, 1948.
Gruening, Martha. "The Negro Renaissance." *Hound and Horn* 5 (1932):
      504-514.

Hansell, William Harold. "Positive Themes in the Poetry of Four Negroes: Claude McKay, Countée Cullen, Langston Hughes, and Gwendolyn Brooks." Ph.D. dissertation, University of Wisconsin, 1972.

Isaacs, Harold R. "Five Writers and Their African Ancestors." *Phylon* 21 (1960): 243-265.

Jackson, Blyden and Louis Rubin. *Black Poetry in America*. Baton Rouge: Louisiana State University Press, 1974.

Killens, John O. "Another Time When Black Was Beautiful." *Black World*, November 1970, pp. 20-36.

Moore, Gerald. "Poetry in the Harlem Renaissance." In *Black American Writer*, vol. 2, edited by C.W.E. Bigsby, pp. 67-76. Baltimore: Penguin Books, 1969.

O'Daniel, Therman B., ed. *Langston Hughes: Black Genius; a Critical Evaluation*. New York: William Morrow, 1971.

Prowle, Allen D. "Langston Hughes." In *The Black American Writer*, vol. 2, edited by C.W.E. Bigsby, pp. 77-87. Baltimore: Penguin Books, 1969.

Starke, Catherine Juanita. *Black Portraiture in American Fiction: Stock Characters, Archetypes, and Individuals*. New York: Basic Books, 1971.

Turpin, Waters E. "Four Short Fiction Writers of the Harlem Renaissance—Their Legacy of Achievement." *CLA Journal* 11 (1967): 59-72.

Wagner, Jean. *Black Poets of the United States from Paul Laurence Dunbar to Langston Hughes*. Urbana: University of Illinois Press, 1973.

HURSTON, ZORA NEALE (1903-1960)

Bone, Robert. "Zora Neale Hurston." In *The Black Novelist*, edited by Robert Hemenway. Columbus, Ohio: Charles E. Merrill, 1970.

Bontemps, Arna, ed. *The Harlem Renaissance Remembered*. New York: Dodd, Mead, 1972.

Davis, Arthur P. *From the Dark Tower: Afro-American Writers 1900-1960*. Washington, D.C.: Howard University Press, 1974.

Gloster, Hugh M. *Negro Voices in American Fiction*. Chapel Hill: University of North Carolina Press, 1948.

Jackson, Blyden. "Some Negroes in the Land of Goshen." *Tennessee Folklore Society Bulletin* 19 (1953): 103-107.

Neal, Larry. "Eatonville's Zora Neale Hurston: a Profile." In *Black Review No. 2*, pp. 11-24. New York: Morrow, 1972.

Turner, Darwin T. *In a Minor Chord: Three Afro-American Writers and Their Search for Identity*. Carbondale: Southern Illinois University Press, 1971.

Walker, Alice. "In Search of Zora Neale Hurston." *Ms.* 3 (March 1975): 74-79.

JOHNSON, JAMES WELDON (1871-1938)

Adelman, Lynn. "A Study of James Weldon Johnson." *Journal of Negro History* 52 (1967): 128-145.

Bronz, Stephen H. *Roots of Negro Racial Consciousness; the 1920's: Three Harlem Renaissance Authors*. New York: Libra Publishers, 1964.

Davis, Arthur P. *From the Dark Tower: Afro-American Writers 1900-1960*. Washington, D.C.: Howard University Press, 1974.

Davis, Charles T. "The Heavenly Voice of the Black American." In *Anagogic Qualities of Literature*, edited by Joseph P. Strelka, pp. 107-119. University Park: Pennsylvania State University Press, 1971.

Fleming, Robert E. "Irony as a Key to Johnson's *The Autobiography of an Ex-Coloured Man.*" *American Literature* 43 (1971): 83-96.

Ford, Nick Aaron. "The Negro Author's Use of Propaganda in Imaginative Literature." Ph.D. dissertation, State University of Iowa, 1945.

Jackson, Blyden and Louis Rubin. *Black Poetry in America*. Baton Rouge: Louisiana State University Press, 1974.

Millican, Arthenia Bates. "James Weldon Johnson: In Quest of an Afrocentric Tradition for Black American Literature." Ph.D. dissertation, Louisiana State University & Agricultural & Mechanical College, 1972.

Starke, Catherine Juanita. *Black Portraiture in American Fiction: Stock Characters, Archetypes, and Individuals*. New York: Basic Books, 1971.

Wagner, Jean. *Black Poets of the United States from Paul Laurence Dunbar to Langston Hughes*. Urbana: University of Illinois Press, 1973.

LARSEN, NELLA (1893?-1963)

Bontemps, Arna, ed. *The Harlem Renaissance Remembered*. New York: Dodd, Mead, 1972.

Davis, Arthur P. *From the Dark Tower: Afro-American Writers 1900-1960*. Washington, D.C.: Howard University Press, 1974.

Ford, Nick Aaron. "The Negro Author's Use of Propaganda in Imaginative Literature." Ph.D. dissertation, State University of Iowa, 1945.

Gloster, Hugh M. *Negro Voices in American Fiction*. Chapel Hill: University of North Carolina Press, 1948.

MCKAY, CLAUDE (1889-1948)

Arden, Eugene. "The Early Harlem Novel." *Phylon* 20 (1959): 25-31.

Bontemps, Arna, ed. *The Harlem Renaissance Remembered*. New York: Dodd, Mead, 1972.

Bronz, Stephen H. *Roots of Negro Racial Consciousness; the 1920's: Three Harlem Renaissance Authors.* New York: Libra Publishers, 1964.

Christian, Barbara. "Spirit Bloom in Harlem: The Search for a Black Aesthetic During the Harlem Renaissance; the Poetry of Claude McKay, Countée Cullen, and Jean Toomer." Ph.D. dissertation, Columbia University, 1970.

Collier, Eugenia W. "I Do Not Marvel, Countee Cullen." *CLA Journal* 11 (1967): 73-87.

Conroy, Sr. M. James. "Claude McKay: Negro Poet and Novelist." Ph.D. dissertation, University of Notre Dame, 1968.

Cooper, Wayne. "Claude McKay and the New Negro of the 1920's." In *The Black American Writer*, vol. 2, edited by C.W.E. Bigsby, pp. 53-65. Baltimore: Penguin Books, 1969.

Davis, Arthur P. *From the Dark Tower: Afro-American Writers 1900-1960*. Washington, D.C.: Howard University Press, 1974.

Ford, Nick Aaron. "The Negro Author's Use of Propaganda in Imaginative Literature." Ph.D. dissertation, State University of Iowa, 1945.

Gloster, Hugh M. *Negro Voices in American Fiction*. Chapel Hill: University of North Carolina Press, 1948.

Gruening, Martha. "The Negro Renaissance." *Hound and Horn* 5 (1932): 504-514.

Isaacs, Harold R. "Five Writers and Their African Ancestors." *Phylon* 21 (1960): 243-265.

Jackson, Blyden and Louis Rubin. *Black Poetry in America*. Baton Rouge: Louisiana State University Press, 1974.

Kent, George E. "The Soulful Way of Claude McKay." *Black World*, November 1970, pp. 37-51.

Lederer, Richard. "The Didactic and the Literary in Four Harlem Renaissance Sonnets." *English Journal* 62 (1973): 219-223.

Lopez, Manuel D. "Claude McKay." *Bulletin of Bibliography* 29, No. 4 (1972): 128-134.

Moore, Gerald. "Poetry in the Harlem Renaissance." In *The Black American Writer,* vol. 2, edited by C.W.E. Bigsby, pp. 67-76. Baltimore: Penguin Books, 1969.

Starke, Catherine Juanita. *Black Portraiture in American Fiction: Stock Characters, Archetypes, and Individuals.* New York: Basic Books, 1971.

Turpin, Waters E. "Four Short Fiction Writers of the Harlem Renaissance—Their Legacy of Achievement." *CLA Journal* 11 (1967): 59-72.

Wagner, Jean. *Black Poets of the United States from Paul Laurence Dunbar to Langston Hughes.* Urbana: University of Illinois Press, 1973.

THURMAN, WALLACE (1902-1934)

Arden, Eugene. "The Early Harlem Novel." *Phylon* 20 (1959): 25-31.

Bontemps, Arna, ed. *The Harlem Renaissance Remembered.* New York: Dodd, Mead, 1972.

Davis, Arthur P. *From the Dark Tower: Afro-American Writers 1900-1960.* Washington, D.C.: Howard University Press, 1974.

Ford, Nick Aaron. "The Negro Author's Use of Propaganda in Imaginative Literature." Ph.D. dissertation, State University of Iowa, 1945.

Gloster, Hugh M. *Negro Voices in American Fiction.* Chapel Hill: University of North Carolina Press, 1948.

West, Dorothy. "Elephant's Dance." *Black World,* November 1970, pp. 77-85.

TOOMER, JEAN (1894-1967)

Ackley, Donald G. "Theme and Vision in Jean Toomer's *Cane.*" *Studies in Black Literature* 1 (1970): 45-65.

Bontemps, Arna, ed. *The Harlem Renaissance Remembered.* New York: Dodd, Mead, 1972.

Christian, Barbara. "Spirit Bloom in Harlem: The Search for a Black

Aesthetic During the Harlem Renaissance: the Poetry of Claude McKay, Countée Cullen, and Jean Toomer." Ph.D. dissertation, Columbia University, 1970.

CLA Journal 17 (June 1974). Ten articles devoted to the author (by Blackwell, Blake, Dillard, Fisher, Kramer, Kopf, Matthew, McCarthy, Riley, and Turner).

Davis, Arthur P. *From the Dark Tower: Afro-American Writers 1900-1960.* Washington, D.C.: Howard University Press, 1974.

Dillard, Mable Mayle. "Jean Toomer: Herald of the Negro Renaissance." Ph.D. dissertation, Ohio University, 1967.

Gloster, Hugh M. *Negro Voices in American Fiction.* Chapel Hill: University of North Carolina Press, 1948.

Goede, William J. "Jean Toomer's Ralph Kabnis: Portrait of the Negro Artist as a Young Man." *Phylon* 30 (1969): 73-85.

Krasny, Michael Jay. "Jean Toomer and the Quest for Consciousness." Ph.D. dissertation, University of Wisconsin, 1972.

Lieber, Todd. "Design and Movement in *Cane.*" *CLA Journal* 23 (1969): 35-50.

Mason, Clifford. "Jean Toomer's Black Authenticity." *Black World,* November 1970, pp. 70-76.

Moore, Gerald. "Poetry in the Harlem Renaissance." In *The Black American Writer,* vol. 2, edited by C.W.E. Bigsby, pp. 67-76. Baltimore: Penguin Books, 1969.

Munson, Gorham. "The Significance of Jean Toomer." *Opportunity* 3 (1925): 262-263.

Reilly, John M. "Jean Toomer: An Annotated Checklist of Criticism." *Resources for American Literary Study* 4 (Spring 1974): 27-56.

Scruggs, Charles. "Jean Toomer: Fugitive." *American Literature* 47 (March 1975): 84-96.

Turner, Darwin T. *In a Minor Chord: Three Afro-American Writers and Their Search for Identity.* Carbondale: Southern Illinois University Press, 1971.

Turpin, Waters E. "Four Short Fiction Writers of the Harlem Renaissance—Their Legacy of Achievement." *CLA Journal* 11 (1967): 59-72.

Wagner, Jean. *Black Poets of the United States from Paul Laurence Dunbar to Langston Hughes.* Urbana: University of Illinois Press, 1973.

BIBLIOGRAPHY OF BIBLIOGRAPHIES

Most of these bibliographies are not concerned specifically with the Harlem Renaissance, but a careful perusal will yield a number of interesting items to the searcher.

Houston, Helen Ruth. "Contributions of the American Negro." *Bulletin of Bibliography* 26, No. 3 (1969): 71-79.

Lash, John S. "The American Negro and American Literature: A Check List of Significant Commentaries." *Bulletin of Bibliography* 19 (1946): 12-15.

———. Part II. pp. 33-36.

Locke, Alain, comp. *A Decade of Negro Self-Expression*. n.p.: John F. Slater Fund, Occasional Papers no. 26, 1928.

Miller, Elizabeth W. *The Negro in America: A Bibliography*. Cambridge: Harvard University Press, 1966.

Turner, Darwin T., comp. *Afro-American Writers*. New York: Appleton-Century-Crofts, 1970.

INDEX

ABOUT THE AUTHOR

Margaret Perry is head of the reader services division at River Campus, the University of Rochester, New York. She received her A.B. degree in 1954 from Western Michigan University and her M.S.L.S. in 1959 from the Catholic University of America. Her special interest is Afro-American literature. Her first book *A Bio-Bibliography of Countee P. Cullen, 1903-1946* was published by Greenwood Press in 1971.